THE GREENING OF A NATION?

*Environmentalism in the United States
Since 1945*

D1125374

HARBRACE
BOOKS
ON AMERICA

SINCE 1945

THE GREENING OF A NATION?

Environmentalism in the United States Since 1945

Hal K. Rothman
University of Nevada, Las Vegas

Under the general editorship of
Gerald W. Nash and Richard W. Etulain
University of New Mexico

Harcourt Brace College Publishers

Fort Worth   Philadelphia   San Diego   New York   Orlando   Austin   San Antonio
Toronto   Montreal   London   Sydney   Tokyo

Publisher	Christopher P. Klein
Senior Acquisitions Editor	David C. Tatom
Product Manager	Steven K. Drummond
Developmental Editor	Pam Hatley
Project Editor	Betsy Cummings
Production Manager	Diane Gray
Art Director	Garry Harman
Electronic Publishing Coordinator	Deborah Lindberg

Cover Image   © Rob Day/SIS

Harcourt Brace College Publishers may provide complimentary instructional aids and supplements or supplement packages to those adopters qualified under our adoption policy. Please contact your sales representative for more information. If as an adopter or potential user you receive supplements you do not need, please return to your sales representative or send them to:

Attn: Returns Department
Troy Warehouse
465 South Lincoln Drive
Troy, MO 63379

Address for Editorial Correspondence: Harcourt Brace College Publishers, 301 Commerce Street, Suite 3700, Fort Worth, TX 76102.

Address for Orders: Harcourt Brace & Company, 6277 Sea Harbor Drive, Orlando, FL 32887-6777. 1-800-782-4479, or 1-800-433-0001 (in Florida).

Library of Congress Catalog Card Number: 97-71644

ISBN: 0-15-502855-3

Printed in the United States of America

8 9 0 1 2 3 4 5 6 066 0 9 8 7 6 5 4 3

For my family,
Lauralee, Talia, and Brent

CONTENTS

Chapter 7
ARCH VILLAIN, HERO, OR CONSENSUS-BUSTER? JAMES WATT AND THE END OF AN ERA   169

Chapter 8
EARTH DAY REVISITED: A GLOBAL ETHOS OR A POLITICAL PROBLEM?   193

PREFACE

Environmentalism is one of the most important new dimensions to appear in American society in the post-1945 world. Part social movement, part manifestation of the increasing affluence and privilege of American society and different from the conservation movement that preceded it, environmentalism took center stage in the transformation of the values and mores of the second half of the twentieth century. A product of prosperity of the post-war moment, that marvelous aberration between 1945 and 1974 when more Americans did better economically than at any time before, environmentalism began as a radical attack on the dominant, development-oriented current of post-war American society and soon became a middle ground, a universal goal as Americans came to believe in an amorphous right called "the quality of life." As such, environmentalism became a value widely professed but to which people paid only lip service. In this limited loyalty, environmentalism revealed both the power of social movements in a media-driven culture and conversely, their limits. As a reflection of the changes in American society as a whole, environmentalism became paradoxical. It became a secular religion, but like most American religions, its adherents were many and its faithful few.

The Greening of a Nation? explores the more than fifty years since the end of World War II when environmentalism became a recurrent theme in American life. It had to change radically to meet the challenges of the post-war era. In that transformation, David Brower, the principal in the Sierra Club, played the primary role, taking conservation from its elite roots and transforming it into to a more general, more political movement. In the aftermath of the Echo

Park controversy of the early 1950s, the environmental movement gained political power and strength. This influence reached its peak with the passage of the Wilderness Act of 1964 and the Endangered Species Act of 1973, both the product of a bipartisan consensus in Congress that enjoyed widespread support among the public. The National Environmental Policy Act of 1970, which authorized the creation of the Environmental Protection Agency, was another signal moment, as was the first Earth Day. This environmentalism was predicated upon the increasing affluence of American society and a widespread belief in the idea that "quality of life" was a right. It responded to the feeling that industrialization had consequences, but modern people should not have to bear the burden of pollution, smog, and hazardous waste.

The sense of privilege that dominated the values of environmentalism became increasingly difficult to sustain as the conditions of American economic life began to change. After 1974, the real value of the wages of working people began a more than twenty-year decline in purchasing power, setting up a battle between the tenets of environmentalism and the economic conditions of working life. In an era of prosperity, it was easy to place the goals of environmentalism beside an expanding economy. As the economy slowed, these values overlapped. The result was first a fracturing of the bipartisan consensus and later the polarization of the dialogue about environmental issues. In this way, the greening of the nation remains an incomplete process. Americans have learned to profess environmentalism, but their actions show a different reality. They embrace environmentalism when it is convenient and inexpensive, but when it challenges the comforts to which they are accustomed, they ignore or avoid it. On an intellectual level, Americans accept the tenets of environmentalism; their actions reveal a more complicated system of beliefs that speaks volumes about the values of Americans and the culture they have created.

ACKNOWLEDGMENTS

No book can be written without various kinds of support, emotional and intellectual, and this one is no different. A range of colleagues, friends, and graduate students offered their input and support. Gerry Nash and Dick Etulain, editors of the series in which this volume appears, provided important and wise guidance in their critiques of the manuscript. Char Miller read and critiqued a portion of the manuscript, adding his fine touch to the work. Richard Mingus, Cathleen Loucks, and Brian Frehner also offered their insights on all or part of the manuscript, contributing greatly to its shape; all have since gone on to much better things. Barbara Chamberlain gave a fine edit to a large portion of the manuscript. Tom Latousek chased down photos from the slimmest of leads. All of them contributed to shaping this project; I am grateful for their help.

As always, my family deserves my deepest gratitude. My wife Lauralee has become accustomed to the long hours I spend researching and writing, to my frequent travels, and she bears my absence and the responsibilities that accompany it without complaint. Our children, Talia and Brent, are the most welcome interruptions of work I've ever experienced. The three of them have helped me remember what is really important in life. This one, like all the others, is for them, with my deepest love and affection.

Introduction

—

ABUNDANCE, SCARCITY, OPTIMISM, AND PROSPERITY

The end of the Second World War caused Americans to collectively heave an immense sigh of relief. The sheer joy embodied in the response of all people to this finale to a long, dark, fearful period masked the immense transformations wrought by the war. Americans had redistributed demographically, with millions moving from rural areas to cities in search of war-related employment. A significant portion traveled west to California; others migrated from the deep South to the industrialized cities of the American North. Still more went from farms to towns and cities such as Wichita, Kansas, where factories built airplanes, and Peoria, Illinois, with its huge equipment plants. Most Americans experienced greater prosperity than they had before the war, and in 1945 only those who had lost loved ones in the war were prepared to trade in their new lives for the ones they had before the attack on Pearl Harbor in 1941.

The war produced a climate of optimism in the nation. Americans had created and then become the engine that conquered fascism. They built an enormous physical plant to support that effort, developing a stunning array of technologies, culminating in the atomic bomb, while revolutionizing production and transportation scheduling. They knew, instinctively and fundamentally, that they had crossed barriers that no group of humans had ever before succeeded in crossing; their ambivalence about the power demonstrated by the two atomic bombs dropped on Japan told them as much. Americans had become the people of the technological solution to all classes of problems, and they had faith in the prosperity that their ingenuity would bring. In the words of David Potter, a noted historian of the time, Americans were at their core a "people of plenty."

That optimism was short-lived. After their successes in the war, Americans returned to continue their development of the North American continent in the fashion that generally had been common in U.S. history: progress, often merely for its own sake, equated with unbridled good. But very quickly cracks appeared in the armor of this steel-polished invincibility. Beginning in the early 1950s and continuing throughout the next two decades, the nation underwent a revolution in values during which the concept of progress lost some of its primacy. Americans challenged the assumptions by which their forebears lived while remaining dependent on the same economic and cultural mechanisms. A series of events—beginning with the attempt to inundate Dinosaur National Monument behind the proposed multipurpose Echo Park Dam in the 1950s and including the publication of Rachel Carson's *Silent Spring* in 1962—sparked first uneasiness, later suspicion, and finally outright hostility to an unthinking allegiance to progress in many quarters of American society. People throughout the nation began to see and appreciate intangible reasons for using the physical world with more care. Soon after, they sought codification of these objectives in the way American society conducted its business.

This move through the system, typical of middle-class revolutions in the United States, spawned an immense body of law and policy directed at the goal of regulating the physical world—what has become in the American lexicon the "environment." Legislation such as the Wilderness Act of 1964, the National Environmental Policy Act of 1970, the Endangered Species Act of 1973, and the revisions to the Clean Air Act of 1977 reflected a new kind of policy-making and lawmaking in American history. Unlike most turn-of-the-century Progressive Era-legislation directed at conservation goals, these laws did not have mere efficiency as their objective. Instead they sought preservation, compliance with standards, and ultimately remediation when those standards were violated. Part of a larger revolution in American culture, these laws reflected not only the abundance of the immediate postwar period, but also the widespread social optimism of the 1960s and early 1970s.

These changes in attitude spurred a revolution in thinking about the issues of the physical world. Conservation—the idea of efficiently using resources in a manner to further the goal of "the greatest good for the greatest number in the long run," in the words of one of the turn-of-the-century founders of the movement, W. J. McGee—was a legacy of the Progressive era of the early twentieth century. It sought to wisely utilize resources, setting aside places that could not be harnessed by the technologies of the day. The spectacular mountaintops of Mount Rainier National Park and the high-elevation Yellowstone region were typical. Conservation had a muscular presence on the American political, social, and cultural stage at the outset of the century but had begun to decline by the 1930s. By 1945, conservation as a political force was moribund, its embrace of orderly progress paradoxical, and many of its concerns archaic. Mid-century conservationists had become a special-interest group, failing to recognize that the changes in American technological capabilities put at risk even the mountaintop paradises they treasured.

The transformation of conservation into environmentalism gathered momentum during the battle over the Echo Park Dam and rapidly exploded across the political and cultural landscape. Environmentalism gained credence as a result of the 1960s optimism of American society—its sense that all problems could be solved by the application of money and ingenuity and its fervent belief that individuals and their desires could make a difference in a technological society. It flourished as Americans ceased to trust their institutions, as government appeared first corrupt and then, in the aftermath of the Watergate scandal that toppled

President Richard M. Nixon, venal. Environmentalists could place themselves in the vanguard of watch dogs protecting the public interest.

But changes in American society following the Vietnam War and the Organization of Petroleum Exporting Countries (OPEC) oil embargo of 1973–1974 put a significant dent in the entire set of beliefs and assumptions that supported not only environmentalism, but also traditional American ideas of an expanding economy that offered more for everyone. Beginning in 1974, the real wages of American workers began an inexorable twenty-year downward spiral. In the early 1980s, jobs in the traditional industrial sector of the economy began to disappear at an alarming rate. The steel industry was among the first to collapse, the American auto industry lost much of its share of the market to foreign competitors, and layoffs in formerly secure, well-paying blue-collar industries became common. With the loss of jobs came first a vague sense of insecurity, then a widespread social malaise, as President Jimmy Carter labeled it in the late 1970s, and finally a loss of the optimism that had been characteristic of American society. The United States was a changing place, its people less confident than they had been since the Great Depression of the 1930s, its workers less sure of the future of their jobs and unable to find new ones at commensurate pay. The deep-seeded national belief in the promise of prosperity for all was muddied by the events of the previous decade.

During the 1980s and 1990s the idea of protecting the environment at all costs—a product of affluence, abundance, prosperity, and optimism—was under attack as Americans saw the decline in their standard of living as more than a temporary setback and began to perceive the shrinking opportunities for themselves and their children's futures. A different kind of scarcity—a scarcity of opportunity—entered the national dialog, and it inspired a new politics of vindictiveness. Americans feared the future as they never had before, a fear that presented a genuine challenge to the ideas and values of the prosperous decades of the 1950s, 1960s, and 1970s.

This change in direction began with the presidential election of Ronald Reagan in 1980 and gained substantial momentum from the Republican sweep of Congress in 1994. In this formulation of a zero-sum world, where gains accruing to any segment of the population were perceived as coming at the expense of another segment, protection of the environment and economic opportunity became cast as adversarial concepts, a turn of events that may well foretell an end to the kind of environmentalism that characterized much of the second half of the twentieth century.

In this transformation of national priorities is the crux of both the successes and the failures of the American environmental movement. In the post-Chernobyl world, it is impossible to ignore the risks that accompany our lifestyle of convenience. Yet Americans crave the advantages that stem from technology, embrace the stone-washed jeans that drain the water table of the western Navajo reservation, utilize the shrink-wrapped packages and latex gloves demanded by the age of AIDS, and cannot live without the cheap electric power still delivered by impounding the waters of nearly every river in the western part of the nation and always promised by the nuclear industry.

As a nation we want convenience and abundance, but we want it without risk. Environmental protection was designed to mitigate that risk, to measure it and make it tolerable, to guarantee a minimum level of quality of life. That assurance comes with its own set of costs, which Americans tolerate in varying degrees, often depending on their economic situation and their perception of the future. When people perceive limits on their ability to succeed, particularly in material terms, they become more willing to accept greater risk to their health and society if that risk provides them with the money to purchase the amenities they crave. In effect, Americans have shown a tendency to be "green" when it is inexpensive—economically, socially, and culturally—but a reluctance to collectively sacrifice convenience and even the smallest of material advantages to assure a "cleaner" future. This is the paradox of the history of the environmental movement: its call, its challenges, and its limits rolled into one.

Chapter 1

THE QUIET AFTERGLOW: ENVIRONMENT AS AN UPPER-CLASS PHENOMENON

In the years immediately following World War II, the issue of "conservation," as it was then called, had receded far from the consciousness of American society. After the war, the nation embarked on an economic, social, and, within the boundaries of the nation, geographic expansion that transformed the demography and patterns of living of most Americans. Life improved for nearly everybody as new jobs, highways, and other economic opportunities kept many of those who had migrated to cities in their new locations and encouraged others to leave worn-out farms and otherwise marginal economic existence in rural America for the promise of growing cities. Minorities such as African Americans received long-awaited opportunities, first in the military and then, in a symbolic more than a quantitative way, in major league baseball. Later, as a result of legal decisions enforced by the federal government and encouraged by the widespread activities of the civil rights movement, changes followed in education and social arenas. Despite resistance to social change, a new era seemed to be dawning. Once again, the United States became the land of the new; old barriers in social, economic, and cultural life toppled in the hectic postwar years. Within two decades of the end of World War II, nearly everything about American life had been altered.

The nature of the postwar world hastened the culmination of a number of trends with long histories in American society.

Clearly, the war helped inaugurate the civil rights movement, as many Americans became increasingly conscious of the predicament of African Americans in their midst, recognizing the incongruity of fighting a war against fascism and oppression when legal discrimination still existed within their own nation. The social and economic roles of women also changed as a result of the war. Although many women returned either to the home or to lower-paying, lower-status jobs after their stints in the defense industry during the war, all the "Rosie the riveters," as the women in the wartime industrial workplace were called, paved the way for future generations of American women to stake their claim to employment opportunity and social equality. The walls of the pink ghettos of teaching and nursing began to crumble. The battle for "freedom" of peoples, ethnic groups, and nation states all around the globe fought in World War II, became a catalyst of the individual rights revolution in the United States. Those who collectively fought fascism advanced the idea of rights in a manner that later prompted their children to embrace individual rights above social goals at home. World War II kicked off the conceptual transformation of American society.

THE POSTWAR WORLD

Conditions in the United States after the war also accelerated the pace of change in daily life. People worked longer hours, had more spending money as a result of the shortage of consumer goods during wartime, and had more and different ways to spend it. American social institutions such as McDonald's restaurants developed in the years following the war. They reflected the growing need for faster ways of doing everything from commuting to eating that came to dominate the postwar world. Americans wanted more, and they wanted it faster; successful entrepreneurs and business leaders in the postwar era prospered when they remembered this axiom and incorporated it into whatever they sold the public.

The years that immediately followed 1945 also saw the acceleration of development in both urban and rural areas of the nation. Cities expanded into metropolises as new suburban housing areas were built along the tentacles of highways that protruded from urban cores. The most famous of these communities, Levittown on Long Island, outside New York City, was the start of an extensive boom that saw the nation's 114,000 new housing starts of 1944 climb to 937,000 in 1946 and 1,183,000 in 1948. In 1950 construction began on nearly 1.7 million single-family homes. Many of these were along the lines of the original Levittown homes: 720- to 1,200-square-foot units with two bedrooms and one bath on a concrete slab that took up only 12 percent of a 60 x 100-foot lot. Such homes did not provide a great deal of space, but it was more than that to which most American families of the time were accustomed.

Home ownership also provided a level of financial security that vast numbers of American families had never before experienced. Before the war, home ownership had been limited to a small segment of the American population—the middle and upper classes. Workers and small merchants in urban areas rarely owned single-family dwellings; workers usually rented apartments, and fortunate merchants owned the building in which their store was located and lived above it, sometimes with their adult children and families in other apartments in the same structure. No industry suffered more from the Great Depression and wartime shortages than housing; the decline in housing starts began in 1926, and the industry remained at low levels throughout World War II. But as the birthrate began to climb during what has become known as the baby boom and as people's expectations soared alongside, home ownership became an important personal and social goal that entrepreneurs strove to meet.

Using a process modeled on Henry Ford's assembly line for automobiles, developments like Levittown were built at an astounding rate. By July 1948, 180 houses each week, or thirty-six each work day, were being completed. When the first Levittown was completed in 1951, it contained more than seventeen thousand homes and eighty-two thousand residents. The prices were affordable: about two years' wages for the average family, well within the reach of employed veterans and most other workers. These suburbs were different than their streetcar predecessors: they took advantage of the growing American obsession with roads and highways, and they provided people with a private, if sometimes cookie cutter-like, residence of their own. This fulfilled a conceptual dream for Americans, who equated private property with independence and success.

The development of Levittown foreshadowed and typified the growth of other areas adjacent to major metropolitan communities. Beginning in 1950 and continuing over the subsequent thirty years, 75 percent of the country's largest cities lost population. In the same period, 83 percent of the nation's growth occurred in the suburbs. Los Angeles expanded into the San Fernando Valley with astonishing ferocity, transforming the orchards and farms created by water taken earlier in the century from eastern California's Owens Valley into the homes of first thousands and later millions of people. Philadelphia, Chicago, Detroit, Memphis, and other major cities began to sprawl into surrounding agricultural land, swallowing whole anything within easy commuting reach. By 1970, more Americans lived in suburbs than in cities. These concentric rings of homes and businesses had an impact on the lands upon which they sat as well as those around them as people and their automobiles came and stayed in places that before had been rural, remote, and far more difficult even to visit. The aspirations of the postwar world had their first impact on the land that was transformed to create the homes, roads, stores, and later shopping centers that came to characterize the era.

Driving the new market for housing was an economic boom unparalleled in American history. To those who left the military with the federal and state benefits of wartime service, the world was truly their oyster; the option of government loans to finance housing, funds to support an education, and other mechanisms offered opportunities on a scale that no generation of Americans had ever before experienced. In an expanding economy, utilizing more and more natural resources, there appeared to be opportunities for everyone. The aerospace industry—a colloquialism for the vast research-driven military-industrial complex that fueled the development first of California, later Texas, and finally much of the remainder of the Sun Belt and the West—was only the most evident of transformative industries. In Detroit, the soaring demand for automobiles produced more high-paying skilled and unskilled jobs, and people capitalized on them. No one wanted to be left behind in a growing economy, and all set their sights as high as they could imagine. After the war, male and female Americans of every race expected to live better; it was a right they earned in battle: overseas and on the home front.

The postwar economic boom that began as the economy was reconverted for peacetime purposes continued and even accelerated the explosive growth of the war era. More raw materials were necessary as consumer goods replaced weapons as the staple products of American industry. The more widely available range of goods used processes developed in the war, bringing entirely new lines of sleek, exciting products to market. With the pent-up demand for goods created by restrictions during the war and with the money saved from wartime employment burning holes in their pockets, Americans crowded into the marketplace to sample the fruits of their economic and military might. Besides the homes that Americans purchased with a devouring appetite, cars, washing machines, refrigerators, and other "big ticket" items left stores in the possession of their smiling buyers as fast as they could be made.

THE ENVIRONMENTAL CONSEQUENCES OF POSTWAR GROWTH

The demand for consumer products and durable goods created a revolution in production. Vast quantities of timber were necessary to build homes, while immense amounts of fuel had to be available to power cars and the trucks that carried products across the country along the brand new four-lane highways, called interstates, begun during the 1950s. New chemical, technological, and commercial techniques allowed greater consumption of all kinds of products but also created larger amounts of new kinds of waste. As it had in the past, the expansion of the economy, coupled with new processes and techniques, led to growing problems in the management of by-products of industrialization. There was a downside to rapid economic growth, one measured in the declining quality of air and water and in the vistas of the American landscape.

The industrial activity of the war years had a tremendous impact on the way the nation looked. Prior to the war, industrialization had been largely regionalized in major northeastern cities. A triangle formed by Chicago, Washington, D.C., and Boston contained the majority of the nation's heavy industry. Stockyards and related animal-processing enterprises dotted the Midwest and near-West, but with the exception of ports such as New Orleans, San Diego, Los Angeles, San Francisco, and Seattle, prewar industrialization in much of the rest of the nation offered neither the density nor the vast economic energy of cities such as Chicago and Detroit. The war changed that, accelerating the spread of heavy industry throughout the interior of the nation. Airplane construction, shipbuilding, and the mining and processing of minerals such as the magnesium necessary for light-alloy construction created pockets of industrial prosperity in places as remote as the newly founded community of Henderson, Nevada, outside of Las Vegas, which grew around the Basic Magnesium Inc. facility located there; Spokane, Washington, where Kaiser Industries had a huge plant, and Alamogordo, New Mexico, remade by the military. The war brought the benefits and consequences of industrialization to places that had little prior experience with it.

All of these endeavors had severe environmental consequences that were made worse by the lack of knowledge of the impact of chemical and industrial processes on people and land. During and after the war, sewage flowed untreated into American rivers, industrial waste was simply buried on vacant or rural land, smokestacks filled the air with emissions, and on more than one occasion, the Cuyahoga River that passes through Cleveland caught fire. Despite the problems associated with industrial development, a paradox remained. Wartime activity provided the material that won the war as it created tremendous economic opportunity, especially for unskilled rural people, African Americans, and migrants to California. Wartime industrial activity helped account for the dramatic increase in the importance of oil as a source of fuel not only in the United States, but also throughout the industrialized world. Before the war, the United States was primarily coal-powered. The war began the revolution that made oil the dominant fuel as pipelines and refineries became part of the great industrial expansion that drove the war machine. Refined oil products became the dominant source of fuel on the planet. Oil carried more energy per unit of volume than did coal and was more easily transported and stored. Beginning in 1949, oil began an ascent that took its consumption in the United States from 5.8 billion barrels per year in 1949 to more than 16.4 billion in 1971. General Motors, one of the greatest beneficiaries of the change in fuels, became the most important American corporation as it quickly made more cars than all its competitors combined and amassed a phenomenal amount of power and influence. Powered by the cheap gasoline increasingly coming from abroad, GM cars dominated the landscape and the psyche of success in the United States.

But driving all those cars had consequences. Exhaust emissions began to cloud the sky, producing a combination of smoke and fog called "smog" that became common in American cities. Refined gasoline contained lead, known since ancient history as a damaging and sometimes deadly mineral if ingested or inhaled. Along with that of other potentially harmful chemicals, lead fumes poured from the automobiles that crowded American roads. The cars of the 1940s and 1950s were big and getting bigger—loud contraptions that moved at faster speeds than their prewar predecessors. When Alfred P. Sloan, the chairman of General Motors and the driving force in the automobile industry for more than three decades, decided that postwar Americans wanted styling first and automatic transmissions second in their automobiles, he directed GM to deliver. In 1947 GM even scrapped a prototype of a smaller car, which would have been named the Chevrolet Cadet and would have carried a sticker price of less than $1,000, because its profit margins were too low

Los Angeles has become the epitome of the overcrowded city. The phenomenon of traffic jams, like the one shown here, began in the 1950s and 1960s.

in comparison with larger cars to make the investment in production worthwhile. The invention in 1947 of a high-compression engine that used high-octane gasoline by GM chief of research and engineer deluxe Charles Kettering helped power the trend toward larger, more powerful, energy-oblivious automobiles. Conceptualized and often designed by Harley Earl, whom author David Halberstam has called the "standard bearer of the new age of affluence and abundance," the cars of the late 1940s and 1950s looked gorgeous—sleek, long, and finned—but they burnt gasoline needlessly, packed the roads, and left a haze in the skies with their exhaust fumes. Postwar industrial progress had its discontent built in.

The designers of this rapid pace of industrialization paid little attention to environmental consequences. With a world to rebuild, with fuel abundant even as imports grew annually, and with economic prosperity within the reach of a larger and more diverse segment of the population than ever, there were few reasons to pay attention to the emission-clouded skies, the fouled lakes and rivers, and the increasingly sooty feel of industrial cities. From the point of view of millions of ordinary Americans, there was tremendous benefit to this technological revolution. As they went to work in the expanded industrial economy, in steel mills, chemical plants, weapons facilities, and the numerous other industrial enterprises transformed as a result of wartime innovation, they assumed that their employers would not subject them to untoward risk. For "hydrocarbon man"—author Daniel Yeargin's term for a worker who derived a higher standard of living from the rise in importance of petroleum and its by-products—any side effects were considered part of the price of progress.

Even the social critics of the years that followed World War II paid little attention to environmental issues. Thinkers such as Daniel Bell, David Riesman, and William H. Whyte looked at social interactions as well as at the organization and values of contemporary American society, taking the physical world and both its abundance and sustainability as constant factors. Although they were critical of industrial society, the problems they saw reflected the impact of a rigid, hierarchical society on individuals, not on the planet. Even prescient thinkers such as Betty Friedan, who coined the phrase "the problem with no name" to describe the predicament of unfulfilled housewives of the era, looked only at the psyche of human beings and not at their relationship to the world around them. During the 1950s, people thought about the problems of people, not about the condition of the physical world and the implications of human actions for long-term survival of the species.

CONSERVATION AND THE QUIET AFTERGLOW

Despite the assaults on the physical world by the increased pace of economic development, the protoenvironmental consciousness embodied in the term "conservation" remained the province of elite groups. As suburbs gobbled up land and as companies used more timber, coal, electricity, and other staples of the industrialized world, Americans basked in the glory of their prosperity. Even the leaders of the conservation movement went along with the tenor of the time. Most of them held important positions in their industries, and the majority subscribed to a view that progress and the ethic of conservation—the idea of preserving resources for future generations—were compatible philosophies. Few Americans challenged the dominant ethos of the postwar world, and fewer still were in a position to do anything about the changes in U.S. society.

The powerful constituency that supported the idea of conservation at the turn of the century had wielded great power, headed by figures such as President Theodore Roosevelt, Gifford Pinchot, the first American professional forester and the first head of the U.S. Forest Service, and John Muir, a staunch and vocal advocate of the preservation of nature who expressed his views in strident tones. Through attrition, complacency, and a sense of success, conservationists withdrew from national politics and fragmented into smaller special-interest groups within the broad rubric of conservation. By the 1940s only a few groups with even a pretense of national standing and influence remained. Typical of these was the Sierra Club, a western-based, nature-oriented group dominated by genteel white, upper-middle-class members. Other groups, such as the Izaak Walton League, the Wilderness Society, and the newer National Wildlife Federation, mirrored the Sierra Club's demography and interests.

In 1945 conservation as a political force had descended to its weakest level in the twentieth century. None of the leading organizations had political standing or significant influence on policy-making or national leadership. Conservationists had abdicated the muscular political style of Roosevelt and Pinchot in favor of a limited perspective and an individualist style. Even the cantankerous and irascible Harold L. Ickes, secretary of the interior since 1933 and a powerful force for conservation, had exhausted his political capital in Washington, D.C., and was on his way out of government. The political and cultural climate of the postwar era was different, and the old ways of accomplishing conservation objectives were archaic in an era of different concerns and rapid economic growth. Even with an organizational structure that remained viable, conservation lacked a national vision as well as a clearly expressed stance on what had the potential to become the pressing issues of the day. Most of its leaders and organizations followed the vectors that their organizations had established at the turn of the century, when progress and preservation seemed compatible. They focused on regional or place-specific issues, looking at the mountains instead of the cities, at the so-called pristine places instead of the communities where people lived. Schooled in a different time, conservation had become a classic special-interest avocation.

The Sierra Club served as the prototype of conservation organizations. Founded in 1892 in California by Muir, the noted mountaineer, scientist, and advocate of the preservation of wilderness for its own sake, and by a number of other Californians, the club emerged as the major conservation organization in the nation before 1945. Although Muir, a man of infinite passion for untrammeled nature, was self-taught and often nearly impoverished by choice, most of the other founders of the organization were formally educated and affluent. Robert Underwood Johnson, the editor of *Century Magazine,* an important national magazine early in the twentieth century, served as catalyst for the organization. Stanford University president David Starr Jordan was among the founders, as was attorney Warren Olney, later the mayor of Oakland, California, and scientist Joseph LeConte, a University of California professor regarded as the most influential teacher in the state. The early Sierra Club had it all: power, standing, influence, access to wealth, and a worldview that shared the value system of the time and mirrored its dominant ethos.

This meeting of wealth, power, and education was typical of the Progressive era, when the mechanisms for regulating an unbridled society were put into place. Progressives often came from the old middle class, whose members had their prestige and status impinged upon by the industrial transformation of the late nineteenth century. Their response was to reassert their claims to leadership in American society, not in the gauche economic terms of the Gilded Age, but rather in the emphasis on efficiency and professionalism that characterized the reform climate of the beginning of the twentieth century. In the 1890s Johnson and Muir had begun by seeking national park status for Yosemite, then designated as a state park. What resulted was an organization that anticipated the values of the Progressive era just as reform sentiment gathered momentum across the land. Progressives conferred authority on a class of people with education and expertise instead of on those who possessed merely wealth. Its leaders perceived their objectives as being part of the common good. Personal economic gain was decidedly not their goal. Progressive conservationists saw themselves as moral defenders of the great outdoors and sought to spread that sentiment through activities such as hiking, camping, and similar outdoor experiences.

There was also a built-in arrogance in their view of the world that was common to people of privilege during the late nineteenth and early twentieth century. In general, Sierra Club members were convinced that their way was the best way, that they and people like them were the ones entitled to an opinion on the subject of conservation in the United States. This view, bolstered by the general outlines of American society, the teachings of mainstream churches, and the political system, reflected the class-oriented nature of the Sierra Club's endeavors.

The Sierra Club also embodied a ruggedness directly inherited from Muir. The "High Trip," an annual pack trip to the highest peaks of the Sierra Nevada range begun in 1901 by Will Colby, the club's consummate organization man, typified the dominant cultural dimension of the club's activities. This excursion became the signature event in the life of the club, the defining symbol of its early history. As late as 1950, Sierra Club members were—in the words of Norman Livermore, who went on to become secretary for resources in the California state government during Ronald Reagan's governorship—a fraternity of "rock climber types." Part machismo and part escape from the growth and development of California in which its early leaders so avidly participated, the "High Trip" became the ultimate moment in the annual cycle of the organization. It reflected the values of an organization comprised of mountain climbers, hikers, and campers—all aesthetic recreational users of the outdoors who valued the transformation of society in which they engaged but who also felt a personal need for distance from it in their leisure time. Seizing upon the amateur tradition in the conservation movement and peopled by educated and influential devotees driven by their passion for the outdoors, the Sierra Club carved for itself a primary role in the conservation movement.

For better or worse, that role and the preeminence of the club remained constant until the end of World War II. Its constituency remained largely the same, its leadership drawn from the same class of educated individuals with a yen for public service that typified the Progressives. Although the policies of the club changed repeatedly, its focus on California protected the Sierra Club from the decline of influence that the national conservation movement experienced as well as from changes in American society at large. World War II served as the catalyst for the Golden State's growth. Until the war, California's economy remained provincial; the demands of wartime production ignited growth at a frenetic pace. Before that growth, it was easy to reconcile the role of advocates of progress with that of preservers of wild land typical of so many of the first two generations of club members.

By 1946 the dominant ethos of the club, and indeed that of the entire amateur tradition in conservation, was in peril. The goal of conservation as an ancillary form of progress, of a separation of a pristine natural world from a somehow fouled and human-created world, seemed increasingly anachronistic. In a changing nation, teeming with people of different classes, genders, and races freed from historic limits by the war, the values of this form of conservation were increasingly irrelevant. As it stood in 1945, the Sierra Club represented an earlier time in American society. Its leaders sounded pompous and exclusive, its political clout had demonstrable limits, and its value system seemed outdated. Typical of the conservation movement as a whole, the

Sierra Club needed new tools to succeed in the postwar cultural environment.

THE NEW CONSERVATION

By the end of the war, people who could implement such an agenda had risen to positions of importance in the Sierra Club. Chief among them was David Brower, the man who later became most clearly identified with the change in attitude from conservation to environmentalism in the United States. Brower dropped out of college in 1931, worked for the Curry Company, the concessionaire at Yosemite National Park, and was appointed to his first Sierra Club committee in 1933. By 1947 he was a veteran on the board of the organization and the editor of its official publication, the *Bulletin*. In Brower's *Bulletin,* the revitalization of the Sierra Club tradition and its expansion to meet the conditions of a new time began to take place.

The new focus was the politics of land management. With Brower's insistent coaxing, the Sierra Club began to fashion a new agenda. Wilderness, remote from the goals of the club a generation before, became the first political issue of significance for the club. As a political issue, wilderness offered many advantages to Brower as he sought to push the group toward the more activist role that he favored and that, not incidentally, could help it maintain a resonance in the postwar world. Brower intuitively understood that the old combination of progress as a value coupled with social outings in the wild would not suffice for the organization in a time of rapid development of previously untouched resources. In the immediate postwar era, the Sierra Club needed a strategy that would give it new vitality and organizational capability. Protection of the mountains, loosely codified as wilderness preservation, began to take a place alongside outings in the Sierra Nevadas as distinctive traits of the Sierra Club.

The preservation of wilderness had a constituency different from but closely related to that of the Sierra Club. Since the 1920s,

David Brower, a dominant figure of the Sierra Club in the 1940s and 1950s, spurred the change in attitude from conservation to environmentalism in the United States.

largely at the behest of conservation biologist Aldo Leopold, who later wrote the American environmental classic *A Sand County Almanac,* the U.S. Forest Service had institutionalized the idea of wilderness in its regulations. The Gila National Forest, where Leopold worked, became the location of the first administratively designated wilderness area within the national forest system. Areas as diverse as portions of the Pajarito Plateau outside of

Santa Fe, New Mexico, and the Maroon Bells peaks near Aspen, Colorado, received primitive area designation from the Forest Service prior to 1935.

Even though he left the Forest Service for private conservation work and eventually accepted a teaching post at the University of Wisconsin in 1933, Leopold had an important impact on Forest Service policy long after his departure. He was the first person in the agency to challenge the dominant ethos of timber management, the first to offer an alternative vision of what forests could be and mean. Leopold was a visionary who saw a different world than the one he lived in, and he believed that a new ethic would bring about a better and more sustainable relationship between human beings and the world they inhabit.

After Leopold, the most influential advocate of wilderness had himself been a member of the Sierra Club. During the 1930s, Robert Marshall became the premier American advocate of wilderness. The son of Louis Marshall, who was one of the prominent American attorneys of the early twentieth century and an ardent conservationist, Bob Marshall grew up in a liberal, affluent environment. As was true of Gifford Pinchot, Marshall's father influenced his career; when the younger Marshall enrolled at Syracuse to study forestry, he took his father's ringing endorsement with him to a university program that his father had endowed. After graduation, Marshall joined the Forest Service, becoming one of its most outspoken and prescient critics. Central to his thinking was the concept of protecting wilderness. This he translated into action as the first private organization designed to protect wilderness began.

Along with Leopold and Robert Sterling Yard—a former newsman and the first leader of the National Parks Association who broke with that organization and the National Park Service over the development-oriented philosophy that dominated the early park system—Marshall founded the Wilderness Society in 1935. "The fashion is to barber and manicure wild America," Yard wrote, and in opposition to this trend, the group recognized "the environment of solitude"—wilderness—as an important resource for the human race. The comparison between wilderness as a "mental" resource and coal, timber, and other natural physical resources was distinct. To sell the concept of wilderness in 1930s America required utilitarian packaging.

The Wilderness Society and the Sierra Club shared some goals, but they differed in important ways. The Wilderness Society drew its members from an extremely narrow segment of the conservation movement and did not seek the widespread constituency that the Sierra Club coveted. Instead, it confined its initial aspirations to the small clique whose members served as leaders of national conservation organizations and focused on the national forests, where most of the remaining land that could be defined as wilderness was located. Aldo Leopold, by the middle of the 1940s the leading American advocate of wilderness, was a leader in the organization. His two sons, A. Starker and Luna, followed, as did Bob Marshall's brother, George, after his elder brother died of a heart attack in 1939. The Wilderness Society was a think tank with policy-planning and policy-making implications, far from the "club" style and nature of the Sierra Club.

Although founded to influence government policy, the Wilderness Society only gradually reached its goal. With the aging and diplomatic Yard at the helm, the society moved slowly in its first decade, enjoying a powerful and influential membership but serving more as a place for discussing than for implementing better policy. Yard himself was still a man of the Progressive era, tied to the rules of this earlier time. Only after Yard died in 1945 at the age of eighty-four did the Wilderness Society begin to fulfill the goals that its founders sought.

In the late 1940s it was difficult to convince leaders of the Sierra Club, the Wilderness Society, or any other major conservation organization to play an important role in confrontational politics. Even with such active leadership as David Brower provided, the Sierra Club simply did not respond with any vigor to his calls to defend the wild. Instead, the club remained rooted in the class-based, archaic form of clubbiness that emphasized outdoor experience, not protection. The Sierra Club directed its energies at providing psychic achievement and moral sustenance for its members. Despite its roots in the Progressive era, it did not focus on conservation or preservation in any of the classic senses of either word.

The Wilderness Society shared similar problems. Both organizations contained internal traditions that made them unaggressive when it came to advocating goals in a public arena. As a forum for discussing ideas, the Wilderness Society gained much early acclaim, but translating those ideas into policy was a more complicated undertaking. Without aspiring to a broad constituency, the society lacked an effective public voice and could only attempt to influence policy-makers. Most of the time both the Sierra Club and the Wilderness Society simply supported the federal agencies responsible for land management.

These agencies—the U.S. Forest Service in the Department of Agriculture, and the Bureau of Reclamation, the National Park Service, and the Grazing Service (which became the Bureau of Land Management in 1948), all of which were units in the Department of the Interior—reflected the history of federal administration of public land in the United States. These agencies were created with specific missions that tied them to a range of constituencies. They faced the congressional appropriations process, needed the support of Congress, and sought to meet the needs of their various publics. The approaches of these agencies revealed both the advantages of a strong federal system and the limitations created by the dependence on the institutions of a democratic society.

Since taking responsibility for national forests from the General Land Office in 1905, the Forest Service had served as the lead federal agency in matters of conservation. It embodied a Progressive era vision that placed efficiency and sustainability of timber and grazing resources over time at the pinnacle of its value system. Rooted in the utilitarian ethos of Gifford Pinchot during the great social and cultural changes that followed World War II, its management goals and objectives came under fierce scrutiny.

The Forest Service tried to redefine itself a number of times throughout the 1920s, 1930s, and 1940s, but it remained inextricably tied to its roots. Pinchot and his Progressive era idea of the greatest good for the greatest number in the long run defined the worldview of the agency, even after Pinchot himself publicly repudiated such ideas during the late 1920s and the 1930s. Forest Service leadership slipped a notch as the people who made Pinchot's policy into rigid dogma rose to executive positions. The result was an agency that by 1945 had lost touch with most of its public—with the singular and significant exception of the companies that cut national forest timber. In the view of many, constituencies such as these controlled the agency.

The National Park Service had also gone through numerous changes by the middle of the 1940s. A decade younger than the Forest Service, it had been founded in 1916 with a modern, market-oriented consciousness that reached an initial peak during the 1920s; the genial and outgoing borax millionaire Stephen T. Mather, its first director, and the determined Horace M. Albright, his piranha-like second in command, had seen to that. From its inception the Park Service was in the tourism business, seeking to accommodate larger and more varied numbers of visitors each year. National park areas, like national forests, were great beneficiaries of the development programs of the New Deal in the 1930s. Almost every park area with aspirations to participate in the tourist trade received a visitor center, roads, trails, and other facilities from such programs.

But the great boom of the 1930s masked internal agency problems. During and after World War II, those problems came to the fore. Chief among them was the bifurcated mission of the agency. The Park Service had been founded to preserve the parks and to make them accessible to the public—goals that in 1916 were not inherently incompatible. By 1945 increases in visitation and expansion of the system combined to make ideas of preservation and of accommodation antithetical. Led since 1940 by a preservationist director, Newton Drury—who was the first person to head the agency without rising through the ranks and who formerly served as president of the Save the Redwoods League—the Park Service leaned toward preservation in its policy directives, but it remained an agency led by landscape architects and engineers, an agency possessed of a culture that favored development.

The Bureau of Reclamation had been the greatest beneficiary of the New Deal. Founded in 1902 as the Reclamation Service after passage of the Reclamation Act, the bureau initially floundered. Although its early mission was to make the desert bloom, its direction seemed unclear, and some in Congress called for disbanding the bureau. Beginning with Boulder Dam—as the project now known as Hoover Dam was called when it was first proposed in 1922 on the Nevada-Arizona border—and continuing throughout the New Deal, the renamed agency found a course that gave it a preeminence among federal agencies in the West. The Bureau of Reclamation was best positioned to inherit the mantle of symbolic achievement, the role of the builder of great American technological monuments that testified to mid-century concepts of the national will, as the power to do so passed from private industry to the federal government. Under President Franklin D. Roosevelt and Ickes, the bureau grew from about two thousand employees to more than twenty thousand, many of whom supervised the contracts that became the lifeline for Morrison-Knudsen, Bechtel, Brown and Root, and the West's other important construction and development companies. Dams were built, often regardless of economic feasibility, and an ongoing boom that supported local and regional business and industry with federal dollars began. Despite a period of weakness early in the 1950s, this "forty-year binge" of federal dam-building, as critic Marc Reisner has called it, lasted into the 1970s.

Massive reclamation projects that generated hydroelectric power and also provided water for reclaimed agricultural land became the forte of the Bureau of Reclamation. Beginning with the Boulder Dam on the Colorado River, followed closely by the Grand Coulee Dam on the Columbia River, and swelling to include nearly every major river in the West, dams eventually dotted the West. Delivering water for irrigation and drinking and generating enough hydroelectric power to light every city in the nation and to power myriad industries besides, such projects fit nicely with the development-oriented ethos of the immediate post-World War II years.

Boulder Dam, (now known as Hoover Dam), the first gargantuan Bureau of Reclamation project, set the tone and style for future agency efforts. The 760-foot-tall dam was the greatest engineering feat of its time. When construction began, no one knew if the task could be accomplished. Its completion in 1936 heralded a new era in the West because it showed that even the most irascible of rivers could be harnessed for the needs of urban areas far away. It also granted the Bureau of Reclamation a kind of primacy with senators and representatives. More than any other federal agency, the bureau claimed the expertise that could help huge swaths of Congress accommodate constituents at home. Almost every state west of the Mississippi River had the combination of federal land and demand for irrigation to make use of a bureau project.

WATER AND GROWTH

The significance of the availability of water in the Southwest in particular could not be overestimated. As the city of Los Angeles engaged in one of its growth spurts at the turn of the twentieth century, it effectively seized and drained the water from the Owens Valley in eastern California's Inyo County. As their hopes faded, the farmers of the valley took out an advertisement in the *Los Angeles Times* that read: "We, the farmers of the Owens Valley, who are about to die, salute you." As one salvo in the many battles over water in the arid regions of the nation, the Owens Valley War set the tone of intraregional discussion of water issues for the subsequent decades.

The rules that governed water relations in the arid regions of the country were called the "doctrine of prior appropriation." This system, which in essence meant "first in time, first in right," differed from the riparian rights granted in more humid parts of the country. In the West, ownership of land did not inherently convey the rights to use water that might flow across it, leaving the door open for consolidation of water in the hands of a few. The earliest date that any user could claim as the original time of use provided priority over any subsequent user. Under the doctrine of prior appropriation, someone could not move in upstream and divert water that people downstream were already using.

The city of Los Angeles excelled in this process of consolidation. As the city and its need for water grew, it drained more and more of the Owens Valley. Its need for water led to larger projects, of which the Boulder Dam was the first and most important. The legislation to establish the dam, titled the Swing-Johnson Bill after its sponsors, sent chills through the rest of the intermountain West. The response was the Colorado River Compact, an agreement between western states that adjudicated the water distribution in the Colorado River. In a 1922 U.S. Supreme Court case entitled *Wyoming v. California,* the Court held that states that used the prior appropriation doctrine in internal water allocation, as did all the basin states, were bound by it in interstate disputes if they shared a common water source. This had the effect of giving the water in the Colorado River to California at the expense of the rest of the basin. Faced with the Court's decision and the Boulder Canyon dam bill, the rest of the states sued for peace. The adjudication of the water in the river under the terms of the Colorado River Compact resulted.

With the help of the Bureau of Reclamation, California consolidated its hold on western water in the immediate post-World War II era. As a result of the state's extraordinary growth, Californians began to use greater amounts of the water allocated to them by earlier compacts and court decisions. As the rest of the West began to grow, civic leaders throughout the Colorado River basin could foresee the need for more water in their own districts. The finite amount of water in the region had finally run up against the demands of its expanding population. A new strategy for meeting all the demands was necessary.

In the late 1940s this strategy was almost entirely in the hands of public officials in local, state, and federal government. The Los Angeles Water District had great power, but so did representatives and senators from the intermountain states. The Bureau of Reclamation—its status and position enhanced by the New

Deal—stood ready to help both sides. Development of water resources in this political and cultural context was an assured outcome; the only questions were how and where it would occur.

SUMMING UP

The conservation movement as it stood after World War II had almost no input into issues such as resource allocation and water development. These were the province of government engineers and other scientific specialists who labored in planning capacities and similar positions in federal agencies. Closely tied to the congressional delegations of arid states, the Bureau of Reclamation often found support for its projects on Capitol Hill. The conservation movement remained politically inept. Its focus continued to be on its traditional realm. The decisions regarding the future disposition of resources such as water, which held the key to development in the West, were in the hands of local leaders, the avid foresters of the Forest Service, and the engineers of the Bureau of Reclamation. Although much of the conservation movement was based in the West, its leaders neither noticed nor responded to the changing conditions.

In effect, the management-oriented set of beliefs that typified conservation during the first half of the twentieth century had been subverted by the changing cultural climate. Conservationists had been, first and foremost, oriented toward efficiency; their emphasis on sustained-yield forestry, on making deserts bloom, on promoting game management and other similar ideas reflected the clear idea that humanity and its technologies could create a more useful and productive world for human endeavor. This world would offer more people better homes and supply arid places with sufficient water to grow marketable crops, applying the virtues and advantages of benevolent, state-supported capitalism and technology to the human condition. These were very much the values of the first generation of conservationists, and their approach to the world was one with which their successors were comfortable. It also dovetailed with the strategy of congresspeople and agencies such as the Bureau of Reclamation.

By the 1940s most of the decision-making on such issues had passed out of the realm, and indeed out of the view, of conservationists. The visionaries of the early twentieth century, both in the public and in the various federal agencies, had been replaced by bureaucrats and technocrats, people with small agendas and specific goals who executed the tasks assigned them but shied away from the larger conceptualization so typical of the founding generation of conservationists. Leaders of many federal agencies simply undertook the projects that Congress granted them, neither creating nor shaping policy or vision. This reactive stance left a huge gap; any larger vision of development projects and their comprehensive significance were usually ignored. The result was a process largely driven by local demand, one that responded to the loudest voices.

Conservationists were not among the voices that Congress, state and local governments, and the federal bureaucracy heard in the immediate postwar era. Retaining their faith in technological progress and their belief in the efficiency of the system of organizations established earlier in the century, most conservationists believed that all was well. They did not quickly recognize the changes around them and generally did not anticipate or understand the increasing impact of humans on the places that they felt were special. Drawn from the upper-middle and upper classes, conservationists in the immediate postwar world stood smugly in their drawing rooms, persuaded that the realm they defended was sufficient.

In part, this silence resulted from an intractable problem. Conservationists historically supported the very types of development in which postwar federal agencies engaged. Efficiency and the greatest good for the greatest number in the long run had been watchwords of conservationists throughout the land. But at the turn of the century, conservationists measured only in the tangible economic terms that reflected their belief in scientific measurement. By the end of the war, two significant changes had occurred. The value of efficient development had begun to be challenged in a number of quarters within the federal government as so many dams were built and forests cut that people began to question whether optimal use of every river or every tree was a good idea. Intangible assets— scenery, solitude, and other similar values—began to play a role in the way some people weighed the choice to grow. Development had also greatly expanded, reaching formerly remote places and blurring the distinction between the mountains and the cities. Conservationists could no longer simply assume that the places they cherished would remain untouched.

Yet until the early 1950s conservation remained a special-interest issue in which advocates confined their interest to wild areas. Few were concerned with, for example, the spread of suburbs, the increasing traffic and the emissions that resulted, or other similar issues; instead, advocates supported issues such as the protection of wild land in the backcountry and some kinds of species preservation, offering general support for the policies of the land management-oriented federal agencies. Questions concerning the disposition of the physical world had fallen far from the prominence they enjoyed during the Progressive era. Lacking a national constituency in an era when the luster of progress had only begun to tarnish, advocates of conservation needed a national issue to galvanize mainstream support around their particular issue. The transformation from a marginal voice to a central voice required a catalyst of immense proportions.

Chapter 2

THE ECHO PARK CONTROVERSY AND THE RESURGENCE: FROM THE COLORADO RIVER STORAGE PROJECT TO THE WILDERNESS ACT OF 1964

By the early 1950s the old conservation movement had reached an impasse. It had come miles from its roots in the progress-oriented ethic of the turn of the twentieth century, embracing a broader spectrum of views and approaches than ever before. A protoecological side of the movement existed, largely as a result of the influence of Aldo Leopold, who died fighting a forest fire near his Wisconsin home in 1948, and Bernard DeVoto, a prescient journalist and historian. The efforts of David Brower and other organizers within the loose aggregation of people interested in conservation also contributed greatly to increased interest in the environment. A political side of conservation again began to thrive as it had early in the century. Brower, who was in the process of becoming the dominant figure in the Sierra Club, had become the center of a widening and still loosely defined movement. But the soft gentility of the history of conservation, the narrow, almost elitist base of its membership, and the influence of the older tradition of interested amateurs still persisted and made change come slowly. If leaders who in 1952 sought a more dynamic, more comprehensive movement had looked around, they would have seen the need for a galvanizing event of singular proportion to propel themselves into the new environmental movement that soon took precedence over all existing forms of conservation.

THE BATTLE OVER THE ECHO PARK DAM

The galvanizing event that made the modern environmental movement come of age was the Echo Park Dam proposed as part of the Colorado River Storage Project (CRSP). The project was a chain of dams planned as a way to control stream flow, to allocate water for agriculture, ranching, and increasing urban use, and to create hydroelectric power to support growth in Utah, Colorado, New Mexico, and Wyoming. This one dam among many became a *cause celebré* that captured the attention of the nation and revolutionized conservation in the United States. At Echo Park, conservation was reborn as environmentalism in a struggle that both served as a replay of the conservation controversies of the turn of the century and paradoxically created an entirely different focus for a new and socially and culturally more complex movement. Echo Park was a line drawn in the sand for an emerging national environmental consciousness; it became an actual and symbolic challenge to the direction in which American society was headed as well as the singular event in the history of postwar environmentalism.

The Echo Park project itself was hardly exceptional by midcentury standards. The upper Colorado River basin states' demands for water to support economic development began in the late 1930s and accelerated through World War II and the years that followed. The judicial allotment of Colorado River water in the 1920s favored California, and as upper basin states grew, they sought to reclaim their share of the river before it flowed downstream. The Bureau of Reclamation, builders of the giant Hoover Dam outside of Las Vegas, Nevada, stood ready to implement a plan. Reclamation officials conceived of a ten-dam project for the upper basin, a proposal typical in scale of the dams built in the era when taming rivers in the United States was both sport and mission.

Echo Park, Utah/Colorado border: Plans to create a dam here gave rise to a protest that galvanized the modern environmental movement.

Initially two of the proposed dams were to back water into Dinosaur National Monument on the Colorado-Utah border in a reprise of the creation of the Hetch-Hetchy Dam in California in the 1900s. At Hetch-Hetchy, the supposedly inviolable status of national parks was challenged, and the Hetch-Hetchy Valley in Yosemite National Park was inundated behind a dam to create a dependable public water supply for the city of San Francisco. In the CRSP planning, two dams within national park areas were projected. One, proposed for Split Mountain Canyon in Dinosaur National Monument, depended on the second and was quickly sacrificed to quiet opponents, but the other, slated for Echo Park in the center of the national monument, drew the ire of prominent conservation groups, gradually refashioned to the political activism promoted by David Brower and others. After the battle for Echo Park, conservation had in fact become environmentalism; it took almost a decade for the name to follow, but the terms of the debate over the use of resources became so different in the aftermath of the battle that observers recognized the crossing of a new frontier.

In the heady post-World War II period, when economic growth and increased production were the order of the day, the Bureau of Reclamation's proposals for the CRSP reflected the nation's cultural norms. The New Deal had accustomed the public to a federal presence that supported local and state goals. Since the late 1930s, Bureau of Reclamation officials had been responding to the demands of the upper Colorado River basin states, seeking to provide the water and power that were essential to economic growth. The New Deal made the Bureau of Reclamation extremely powerful among federal agencies. It became a capital development entity that spewed prosperity for local communities in its wake. Jobs during a project's construction phase and later the benefits of electricity were two of the biggest selling points. During the dismal 1930s, few Americans hesitated to cheer when they saw federal agencies, their coffers full of money that created jobs in destitute communities, coming toward them at breakneck speed.

The war strengthened the federal hold on the West. Defense factories increased federal autonomy and local dependence on it. In agencies such as the Bureau of Reclamation, a smug attitude began to prevail. At the height of its power and influence in the postwar exuberance, the bureau was well positioned throughout the administration of Harry S. Truman. Reclamation officials saw themselves as friends of the people and sincerely believed that their own judgment about the needs of communities and regions was correct and true. It was in everyone's interest, officials thought, to harness rivers so that they could be turned on and off like kitchen faucets, so that they could provide the building blocks of regional economic growth.

By the early 1950s the Bureau of Reclamation had selected eighty-one dam sites throughout the West, twenty-seven of which had already been mapped in preparation for construction, most ahead of approval by the Department of the Interior, of which the Bureau of Reclamation was part. Few among the public objected because most of the people in the vicinity of the upper Colorado River expected to gain from the transformation that the dams would bring. With electricity and more plentiful as well as better-regulated water, it seemed that everyone in the region—farmers, ranchers, and urban residents—had a better chance at sustained prosperity.

Bureau of Reclamation officials had forgotten the hard lessons of the Hetch-Hetchy struggle at the beginning of the century that shaped the role of federal agencies in local and regional battles concerning site use. In that struggle over the dam in northern California, the battle was not among regional groups that would be served by the project and that vied for a greater share of the water, but rather between regional water users and a national constituency that believed in the "higher" aesthetic values of Hetch-Hetchy Valley. In the 1900s and early 1910s that constituency, far from the region, placed an intangible value on the beauty of the valley and its status as a national park area and nearly carried off its plan to halt construction of the dam. Although the city of San Francisco won a tough battle in the U.S. Senate and the dam was eventually built, the price was sufficiently high to deter future planners from seeking land within national park boundaries for capital development projects for more than three decades.

But the post-World War II leaders of the Bureau of Reclamation had not been part of the Hetch-Hetchy struggle, and they placed a premium on their own role as providers of civilization's tools. The bureau had become arrogant as a result of its successes. To its leaders, institutions such as national parks were less important than was providing services that the leaders believed were for the common good. In the 1950s their perspective was widely shared; Secretaries of the Interior Julius Krug (1946–1949) and Douglas McKay (1953–1956) agreed that the national parks could be violated if such areas would, as McKay wrote, "produce for the nation values that greatly outweigh those which are [to be] changed or destroyed." In effect, under this policy, a project of national importance could take priority over national park designation in any instance, and national priorities could be quite malleable in the hands of development-oriented leaders.

This philosophy made decisions regarding the sanctity of national parks dependent on the political process in a manner that galled many park advocates. Thanks to the prescient planning of its leaders, the park system had come to be seen as an asset to all of the nation, apolitical in its formation, goals, and structure. The crown jewels of the system—those areas designated as national parks—had been selected in accordance with a loose set of standards that accentuated their status as unique places. They were also selected to transcend local politics, and many influential leaders balked at the idea of making parks political. The concept of national importance put forth in the immediate post-1945 era had become, in most instances, a relative measure—easy to claim and difficult to dispute. Dams in particular could be construed as nationally important in the context of the Cold War, at its height in the 1950s; they were a symbol of the might of American industrialism, and the energy they produced could be harnessed in an instant to fight the Soviet threat. Dams were a linchpin in the growth and development of previously remote areas, creating a stronger economic framework in an era not far removed from severe economic depression. The burden under these postwar standards of national significance fell not to proponents of proposals such as dam projects, but instead to those defending the status quo. In the case of Echo Park, that meant the National Park Service and the slowly invigorating postwar conservation movement.

By the 1950s the Park Service had fallen greatly since its heyday in the 1920s; after the persuasive and territorial Stephen T. Mather and his assistant and later successor, the consummate power broker Horace M. Albright, leadership had been handed to a less-dynamic group. The first generation of Park Service leaders had been frankly accommodationist. They sought to develop the parks for the American public, generally favoring roads and other amenities over preservation. The appointment in 1940 of outsider Newton P. Drury of the Save the Redwoods League as director was a harbinger of a new, more preservation-oriented philosophy, as well as an indication that the conceptual spark that had been at the core of the Park Service at its inception could not be easily found among those near its top a generation later. Drury was the first Park Service director not to rise through the ranks of the agency, testimony to the difficulties inherent in the cross-generational transmission of vision. Groping for a mission in the aftermath of the Depression and World War II and having great difficulty meeting the influx of travelers in the postwar era, the Park Service seemed consumed with internal issues and poorly equipped to fight for its turf. To the Bureau of Reclamation, the Park Service was a far less significant agency, one easily pushed around by this paragon of development.

Nor would a picture of Dinosaur National Monument astride the Utah-Colorado border in the late 1940s suggest that the status quo there was worth protecting. The monument was remote, and it received few visitors. It had been stripped of the purpose for which it had been established in 1915. Paleontologist Earl Douglass, who was working for the Carnegie Museum, found dinosaur skeletons along the Green River in 1909. The eighty-acre site had been designated as a monument in an effort to regulate excavation and to limit Douglass's collecting. The effort failed, and by the middle of the 1920s few skeletons were left in the original quarry. As did many of the parks designated as national monuments in the first four decades of the century, Dinosaur National Monument remained moribund until the late 1930s, when an effort to turn the area into a national park yielded a two hundred thousand-acre-plus national monument oriented toward recreation. Its remote location continued to keep visitor numbers low even after the monument was expanded.

The Park Service and the conservation community banded together to protect this recently enlarged national monument. The conservation movement had already faced its first postwar battles over dams in national parks; in 1948–1949 the Wilderness Society and the National Parks Association (NPA) fought the Bureau of Reclamation's plan to dam the outlet stream of Lake Solitude in the Cloud Peak Primitive Area of the Big Horn National Forest, and along with the NPA, the Sierra Club and the Wilderness Society opposed the Glacier View Dam proposed by the U.S. Army Corps of Engineers for Glacier National Park in Montana. Olaus Murie, then president of the Wilderness Society, developed a strategy of supporting dams outside of parks as a way to protect parks from them. From the perspective of the Park Service and its leaders, concerned more about their domain than other lands, this was a suitable strategy.

But it posed long-term problems for the concept of preservation. Murie, in effect, accepted a de facto designation of "sacred" and "profane" lands—lands marked as having intangible, noneconomic value and lands marked as having only economic utility. His view failed to account for the damage that could be done to so-called sacred lands from outside their boundaries as well as for the importance of lands that, for whatever reason, had not yet received any form of protective sanction. This short-sighted approach was indicative of the narrow scope of the prewar conservation movement, and the aftermath of Echo Park would seriously challenge its efficacy.

In the case of Dinosaur National Monument, the Park Service could not publicly help conservationists battle the dam. After Drury went public with the Park Service's opposition to the Echo

Park project, Krug's successor as secretary of the interior, Oscar Chapman (1949–1953), muzzled the NPS director. At a hearing on the dams on April 3, 1950, Chapman allotted the preponderance of time to project proponents. Soon after, Chapman offered secretarial support for both dams proposed for Dinosaur National Monument, and relations between him and Drury deteriorated. Within a few months, Chapman forced Drury to resign, and a strong voice for preservation was silenced. After a brief interlude during which Arthur E. Demaray, the last of the initial generation of NPS officials, served as caretaker of the agency until his retirement, a new permanent director was chosen. Conrad L. Wirth, a development-oriented landscape architect with twenty years in the Park Service, was named to the position. Wirth had a long history of developing amenities in parks and was usually inclined to find opportunities for development in any situation.

Despite the constraints placed on the agency in charge of Dinosaur National Monument, opponents of the dam persisted in its defense. The conservation community regarded Drury's forced departure as an implicit threat to the entire national park system. Chapman's ruling allowed an open season on parks, opponents of the dam agreed, and they sought to find a way to press their case. Chapman's support of the dam prompted an attempt to spread the message that the parks were under siege to a broader arena. The Colorado River dam package still required legislative approval, and conservation advocates took the battle against the dam to the public. Beginning late in 1950, 78 national and 236 state conservation organizations began to muster their supporters for an all-out assault.

David Brower, by then executive director of the Sierra Club, and Howard Zahniser, his counterpart at the Wilderness Society, took the lead. The largest groups pooled their support in lobbying consortiums such as the Trustees for Conservation, the Council of Conservationists, and the Emergency Committee on Natural Resources, which later became the Citizens Committee on Natural Resources. Direct-mail pamphlets that asked the public: "What is Your Stake in Dinosaur?" and "Will You DAM the Scenic Wildlands of Our National Park System?" appeared in mailboxes across the country. A professionally made color motion picture circulated across the country and was shown hundreds of times. Wallace Stegner, the noted author and historian, edited a book-length collection of essays and photographs dedicated to the proposition that Dinosaur should remain untouched or, in the parlance of the times, "wild." Newspapers and national news and feature magazines addressed the question of the dam at great length. The battle to stop the Echo Park Dam became front-page news.

The form of this battle reflected the changing values of American society. By the early 1950s, in the midst of the Korean conflict and during the rise of red-baiting anticommunists such as Senator Joseph McCarthy, a strong current of dissatisfaction with the status quo began to flow. Progress had been wonderful to Americans, but its cost had been very high. A significant number of people began to wonder, quietly at first, if the establishment of new limits and adherence to existing ones were more than just good ideas.

The battle against the Echo Park Dam also debuted the newly revitalized conservation/environmental movement, more political than at any time since the turn of the century. Since the Progressive era, conservationists had access to influential people and the resources to spread their message; beginning with Theodore Roosevelt, many conservationists had been prominent citizens. Toward the middle of the century, they had become reluctant to use the tools at their disposal. With activists such as Brower and Zahniser in the lead, any hesitancy disappeared, and the new conservation movement aggressively challenged the dam and its backers.

One of the primary arguments that supporters of the dam used to buttress their case reflected long-standing intraregional divisions. Residents of Utah and Colorado believed that without the dam their water would continue downstream unimpeded to California, which used what it needed and let the rest flow into the Pacific Ocean. With California-based organizations such as the Sierra Club taking the lead in fighting the dam, representatives of the upper basin states framed the conflict as an insidious way to maintain the colonial relationship between powerful California and the weaker inland river states. Arousing public opinion against California, even under disingenuous circumstances, was always easy in the Southwest and the mountain West, and it helped create a fictitious division between people of the interior West and Californians. Some who might not have thought the dam a good idea supported it when they saw it framed as a battle with California.

Conservationists responded by stressing their national constituency as well as the broader basis for their objections. The dam in the park was not a regional issue, they insisted time and again. Instead, it embodied the principles of sanctity of national parks as well as the authority of congressional decisions. People across the country opposed the Echo Park Dam. Conservation groups were prepared to demonstrate because of the aesthetic value of the canyon and because of its designation as a national park. Progress is good, opponents of the dam insisted, but not in every canyon and crevasse.

By taking the battle over the dam to the public, conservationists effectively circumvented both the Bureau of Reclamation and congressional supporters of the dam. Preservationists worked quickly because the Senate and House committees making the decisions were loaded with pro-dam western congressmen. The Bureau of Reclamation had strong support, particularly in the Senate, where Joseph O'Mahoney of Wyoming, Clinton P. Anderson of New Mexico, Arthur Watkins of Utah, and Eugene Millikin of Colorado all served. The bureau's driving force, the vaunted cigar-chewing Floyd Dominy, who was already on his way to becoming the most powerful federal bureaucrat in the West, had wide influence and much support on Capitol Hill. Only an unparalleled public outcry could stop the dam.

With mail to Congress late in 1954 running at eighty to one against the dam, the Eighty-third Congress postponed its decision on the CRSP bill. The issues juxtaposed growth in the West and the growing discomfort of people across the nation with rapid and seemingly unstructured change that often appeared to benefit only limited segments of society. There were consequences to actions such as damming a river in a national park, a growing segment of the public believed, and those consequences needed to be considered before the bill should be acted upon. As the Eighty-third Congress adjourned in 1954, Speaker of the House Joseph W. Martin Jr. announced that the controversy about the dam killed the bill's chances for passage. Friends and foes alike awaited the new Congress.

The Eighty-fourth Congress was notable for many things, including the ascendance of Lyndon B. Johnson as majority leader with the Democrats again in control of the Senate, but no issue dominated the session's early days more than the resolution of the Echo Park controversy. Efforts to fashion a compromise failed, and support for the dam's opponents grew. Secretary of the Interior McKay, known by the sobriquet of "Giveaway McKay," had been closely tied to development and timber interests during his tenure as governor of Oregon, and there was every reason to expect Interior to support the dam. Surprisingly, the new director of the National Park Service, Conrad Wirth, voiced his objections to the project. Most expected him to be a friend of the dam. At the Senate hearing, Brower, by then executive director of the Sierra Club, eloquently voiced a range of objections. He exposed the fallacies in the bureau's scientific data, demonstrating that even the calculations of the evaporation rate of water from the pool behind the proposed dam at Dinosaur were inaccurate. Under a barrage of cross-examination questions, Brower offered a powerful challenge to the economic rationale that underlay the dam proposal.

What had once seemed a certainty had become deeply mired in politics. Although Senator Richard Neuberger of Oregon proposed that the Echo Park Dam be eliminated from the CRSP bill, the powerful Senator Arthur Watkins of Utah battled him. In the end, the Senate passed the CRSP bill with the Echo Park Dam intact. The House, more susceptible to pressure because all of its members were reelected every two years instead of every six years, responded in June by passing a bill without provisions for the controversial dam. The battle continued as representatives from Colorado River basin states met on November 1, 1955, in Denver to discuss ways to revive the Echo Park project. One of the main opposing organizations, the Council of Conservationists, placed a full-page open letter in the *Denver Post* that delivered a bold ultimatum: if the Echo Park Dam was put back in the CRSP bill, conservationists would oppose the entire ten-dam project with all the force they could muster by any legal means; if that one dam was eliminated, they would not oppose the rest of the project. Although some charged that the strategy was blackmail, it trapped the proponents of the dam, forcing them to accept the terms, or, in essence, to battle against their own interests. From that point, the resolution of the CRSP without the Echo Park Dam proceeded with comparatively little difficulty. A viable compromise had been reached, and on April 11, 1956, the bill became law.

The battle to stop the dam in Dinosaur National Monument touched a national nerve, raising questions about the smug faith in progress that Americans had embraced. Defeat of the dam became the pivotal moment when Americans questioned the course of their society. Enough of them sought to change its course that the decisions of a powerful federal agency and the support of the representatives in the states in which the project was located were abrogated. This was testimony to the increasing power of both public opinion and of a Congress willing to assert the concept of national interests over parochial home rule. Parks and wild land within individual states had been saved from a dire threat over the objections of representatives of those states. Local values were superseded by national ones as people who lived far from Dinosaur National Monument played an instrumental role in blocking the dam. Many in the conservation movement at the time and many who have written about the controversy since have celebrated the demise of the Echo Park Dam proposal as a major triumph for the conservation movement.

THE PRICE OF SUCCESS

Although it would be impossible to regard the people who fought against the Echo Park Dam as having access to the range of strategies utilized by modern environmentalists, they did develop successful methods that later generations followed. In the 1950s none of the tools that environmentalists have since relied upon was available. There was no law that required an environmental impact statement, no Endangered Species Act, none of the standard measures and legal remedies later developed to challenge federal development projects. But the conservationists-turned-environmentalists had learned the primary rule of success in policy issues in post-1945 America: fight battles in the press where the public can make its own decisions. The support that the environmental groups generated stemmed as much from the closed arrogance of the Bureau of Reclamation as from widespread support of wilderness. By framing national park land as sacred space, conservationists and environmentalists were able to strike a powerful chord with the American public, most of whom may have liked the idea of wilderness but were unlikely to ever go near it.

The definition of park land as sacred space had negative consequences as well. If parks were sacred and inherently protected, other places were not. Conservationists and environmentalists contributed to drawing this clear and distinct line when they gave the western states their ultimatum about the Echo Park Dam. In essence, the groups agreed that if national park land had to be protected, other public lands had to be open for use. Although this perspective won the battle over the Echo Park Dam, it limited the reach of protoenvironmental organizations. The already existing definition of sacred space—specifically national park areas—became contrasted with more-mundane, ordinary, profane space in which people lived every day. By claiming this narrow preserve as their own, conservationists left many equally beautiful and valuable places open to development simply because those places lacked park designation. This shortcoming revealed that the transformation to environmentalism meant more than simply politicizing the values of the conservation movement. It also meant that a new, better-defined and more broadly conceived political agenda with a full-fledged philosophy became necessary to underpin it.

One result of the lack of opposition to other projects in the CRSP was the inundation of Glen Canyon, a one hundred-mile river valley behind the Glen Canyon Dam. This area, a wilderness outside of park or forest boundaries, became the sacrifice that resulted from the effort to save Echo Park. When members of the conservation coalition agreed to other dams in the project, they made a determination based on their supposition that the best places were already reserved, that there were not likely to be hidden gems that had not yet been the subject of conservation legislation. Too late, protoenvironmentalists "discovered" the subtle but spectacular beauty of Glen Canyon. When the gates of the dam closed on January 21, 1963, creating Lake Powell on the Arizona-Utah border, "the place that no one knew"—as Glen Canyon became immortalized in a book edited by Brower and illustrated by Eliot Porter, one of the nation's foremost nature photographers—was inundated.

Like the Hoover Dam before it, the Glen Canyon Dam was testimony to the monumental technological capability of industrial America. It represented technological civilization at its pinnacle, both good and bad. The dam itself overwhelmed the landscape; the pool of water behind it demonstrated the mastery that Americans believed they had achieved over nature. The existence of the dam magnified every trait of modern America, conversely opening those traits to closer inspection by the public.

Later the drowned canyon became a rallying point for the radical wing of modern environmentalism. Brower and Porter masked the problems of compromise by arguing that Glen Canyon was inundated because no one cared enough to engage in another fight. But over time resentment of the damming of the Colorado came to focus on the Glen Canyon Dam; in his 1975 classic book, *The Monkey Wrench Gang*, iconoclastic author Edward Abbey made one of his dam-bursting ecoguerrillas a native of Hite, Utah, one hundred feet below the waters of Lake Powell. The ultimate mission of this unlikely group was to blow up the dam that, in the minds of this constituency, had ruined the lower Colorado River. It was not merely apathy that allowed the inundation of the Colorado River basin, some maintained. In Abbey's formulation, it was the ethos at the very core of a misguided civilization.

The Echo Park battle created a new and expanded constituency for what remained the primary focus of American environmentalism: wilderness. People all over the country became
energized by the struggle, and with the eventual defeat of the
Echo Park Dam, countless Americans believed that a major victory
had been won. They sided with the winners, building momentum for the movement. This activist brand of conservation, which
had begun to transform into environmentalism, soon came to represent one aspect of the search for a usable past to guide a society
increasingly in conflict over the relation between its direction and
its attributes.

LEGISLATING WILDERNESS

The growth of support for environmental issues exemplified in
the Echo Park fight translated into a decade-long struggle for legislation to protect wilderness in the United States. Some of the
reasons were simply pragmatic; post-World War II prosperity and
population growth spurred development, which rapidly consumed thousands of acres of farmland, wild land, and everything
else adjacent to growing and sprawling American cities. Before
the age of rapid transportation there had been a seemingly infinite amount of wild land in the nation, and thus wilderness protection—and in fact even its designation—seemed unnecessary.
As areas that people were accustomed to seeing as wild became
land for tract homes, and as greater numbers of people gained the
mobility and affluence to reach remote places, threats to wild
land became a major issue for environmental groups.

In the lead in this battle was Howard Zahniser, executive
director of the Wilderness Society. A veteran of the Echo Park controversy, Zahniser was a quiet man who knew how to succeed in
Washington, D.C. In the aftermath of the victory over the dam
proposal, an elated Zahniser laid the plans for a national wilderness system sanctioned by federal law. He persuaded Senator
Hubert Humphrey of Minnesota and Representative John Saylor
of Pennsylvania to introduce the first wilderness bills in the second session of the Eighty-fourth Congress in 1956.

The idea of a national wilderness system was a new dimension in a process that had begun in the federal government with the efforts of Aldo Leopold in the 1910s and 1920s. By the end of the 1920s, the Forest Service instituted administratively protected primitive areas, wilderness designated by agency prerogative rather than by law. The founding of the Wilderness Society in the 1930s developed strong support for the concept among individuals in government agencies, but World War II drained momentum from wilderness efforts. Zahniser revived the ideas in the late 1940s, supported by the posthumous publication of Leopold's classic *A Sand County Almanac,* the major ecological philosophy and wilderness treatise of the first half of the century. In the national subsurface discontent with unabashed growth that began to permeate the mid-1950s, wilderness had found its niche.

It was a small niche, but when it opened, people who supported the idea of wilderness began to press their case. The first obstacle was persuading a significant number of congresspeople who supported development that a wilderness bill would not detract from economic growth in their home states. Senators such as Anderson of New Mexico and representatives such as Wayne Aspinall of Colorado were strong advocates of the development of natural resources and had to be made into equally strong advocates of parks and recreational areas. Selling the idea to them seemed possible, if in some situations difficult.

There were important precedents in Congress for supporting a bill to protect wilderness. The growth in visitation in the immediate postwar era overwhelmed the national park system as increased affluence and the time to travel combined to bring millions of Americans to the national parks. By the early 1950s national parks and national forest campgrounds were overrun with visitors and their traces—overflowing garbage cans, litter, tire tracks, cigarette butts, and other forms of refuse and waste. The demands on recreational space were vast, and conditions worsened rapidly. By 1954 Bernard DeVoto, a noted journalist, argued that if the government was not going to adequately fund the national parks, they simply should be closed. Such a radical sentiment did what DeVoto intended it to do: it created an uproar that attracted the attention of the growing conservation-oriented public.

The reason for the rapid degradation of park facilities was hardly a mystery. Much of the system had been built during the 1930s under the auspices of the New Deal and was designed for the more limited visitor load of that era. With the incredible increase in visitors after World War II came crowding, higher maintenance and management costs, a need for more staff members, and every other characteristic of a boom in a service industry. But funding for both the national parks and forests remained constant or increased more slowly than did demand for recreational and educational services. By 1955 national parks were trying to serve 1950s levels of visitors with the resource capabilities of the late 1940s.

Under Wirth, the Park Service had great appeal to congressmen such as Anderson, Senator Alan Bible of Nevada, and other westerners who defined park development as a source of federal funding for their states. Wirth sought development of the parks, something that brought jobs, contracts, and ancillary benefits to western states that were generally in need of more infrastructure. He was the leading proponent of national recreation areas and parkways, both of which created jobs and brought building contracts to congressional districts. Representatives and senators from western states looked at development-oriented agency leaders as kindred spirits. Wirth's vision of the park system matched the goals of a development-oriented Congress.

Out of this alliance came a program called MISSION 66, a ten-year capital development program to refurbish the national parks in time for the fiftieth anniversary of the establishment of the National Park Service, which was to occur in 1966. Park officials remember the program as a windfall; the House and Senate seemed to be competing with each other to give the Park Service more money for new buildings such as visitor centers and permanent homes for staff and for roads, campgrounds, and other developments. Almost every park in the system received some benefit from MISSION 66; its most obvious legacy is the dozens of post office-like visitor centers scattered throughout the national park system.

The federal investment in MISSION 66 reflected the affluence and optimism of the time as well as the increasing importance of environmental issues to the American public. MISSION 66 began as the Echo Park controversy came to an end, as more Americans had time and money to enjoy recreational opportunities. In effect, park amenities became a form of the "pork" that American politicians took pride in bringing home to their district or state. Parks were another way to subsidize states with federal dollars in an era when legislators measured their success by the number of projects they delivered to constituents at home.

It was in this context that Zahniser and the other wilderness advocates sought passage of a bill that precluded land development and offered recreational opportunities only for a few rather than for the great mass of travelers. Even in the positive climate established with MISSION 66, it was a hard sell. Wilderness demanded a different kind of analysis, a different understanding and weighing of values than did development. It required that advocates create in legislators a new pair of eyes with which to see because the passage of a wilderness bill would preserve at least some land in perpetuity from development. For years Zahniser stalked the halls of the Executive Office Building and the Capitol, trying to persuade the men and women of Congress to support a bill that offered them only the gratitude of a small portion of their constituency and a sense of moral righteousness instead of the cheers and dollars to which they were accustomed and that most of them craved.

The indefatigable Zahniser kept the process going, session after session, throughout the late 1950s and early 1960s. Federal agencies assigned to administer the designated wilderness areas that the legislation would create, in particular the Park Service, the Forest Service, and the Bureau of Land Management, were not thrilled with the prospect; from the perspective of these agencies, passage of a wilderness bill would limit rather than extend their discretion over the land they managed. Wilderness designation would restrict the construction of service roads and the use of automobiles, trucks, and other equipment on these lands. To federal agencies, the result appeared to be a more complicated, more expensive form of management that was unlikely to increase their budget allocation. They stalled, seeking to find ways to make wilderness more compatible with existing management strategies.

By the early 1960s the climate in the nation had begun to change in a manner that advanced the cause of wilderness preservation. The ascension of John F. Kennedy to the presidency inaugurated a brief moment that was known as Camelot for its dreamlike faith and optimism. Americans began to believe that their social problems were solvable if only enough money, ingenuity, and effort were applied. Prosperous and expansive, the nation had become a decidedly optimistic place. Kennedy's successor, Lyndon B. Johnson, conceived of a "Great Society" and talked of eradicating poverty in America. Physicians planned the worldwide elimination of diseases. In this climate, seemingly anything was possible.

Environmentalists plugged into the utopian spirit of the time, both at the grass roots and professional levels. The optimism of the time fit neatly with the value system that conservationists-turned-environmentalists and the many new devotees of environmentalism embraced; they shared in the idea that the future could be better, made so by prescient decisions at the moment. Galvanized by what they regarded as the hasty and poorly thought out decisions of the past, these middle-class reformers turned to the remedies of their class: the legislative process and the courts. The urban renewal movement, which changed numerous downtowns by taking down older, aesthetically pleasing buildings and replacing them with post-Bauhaus glass and steel boxes, inspired a backlash that led to the 1966 passage of the Historic Preservation Act. Basking in their affluence and worrying that their heritage was being destroyed, Americans began to take the idea of preservation more seriously than ever before.

Federal agencies also began to professionalize their science divisions in new ways. With the G. I. Bill fueling a tremendous increase in the number of college graduates following World War II and the Korean conflict, there were ample numbers of university-educated scientists to fill the growing number of jobs in the federal service. This professionalization added a trained population that began to reach decision-making positions at precisely the moment when planning became a paramount necessity and vision a much-needed commodity.

The shining example of this vision was the *Leopold Report* of 1963. Authored by A. Starker Leopold, Aldo Leopold's son, and by a number of other professional wildlife biologists, the report evaluated the condition of wildlife in the national park system and advocated an important innovation: a new era of ecologically oriented management. "The major policy change we would recommend," the report stated, "is that [the National Park Service] recognize the enormous complexity of ecological communities and the diversity of management procedures required to preserve them." Pointing out that national park boundaries are political and not ecological divisions and that they in the long run might not be sufficient to protect natural resources within park boundaries, the report made the case for returning the parks to their condition at the time they were first viewed by European visitors. This meant, in effect, their relative condition just prior to the moment of contact and made the case for removing any vestiges of post-Columbian history from the natural areas of the park system.

This vision was in keeping with the cultural climate of the times. The entire idea was fraught with irony; in effect, the *Leopold Report* advocated massive human intervention to eradicate the signs of human presence. Wilderness would be created by people. The very idea of returning the natural world of the parks to an earlier state required tremendous faith in science as well as a powerful combination of wealth and optimism to argue for the funds necessary to support such a transformation. It meant that management of natural resources would grow in the park system, more scientists would be necessary, and the principles of modern scientific disciplines would be applied to federal lands. It also reflected a wilderness-oriented management perspective that was part of the movement for a wilderness system.

The *Leopold Report* was published in its entirety in the Sierra Club *Bulletin,* furthering the strong ties of that organization with the wilderness movement. Under Brower's leadership and in no small part as a result of the Echo Park controversy, the Sierra Club had moved into a leading advocacy role in the development of the wilderness movement. Its biennial wilderness conferences, which began in 1949, had become the preeminent gathering of wilderness advocates. Despite the battles that sometimes raged over the issues and ideas of wilderness, the Sierra Club became an important ground for honing the sentiments that supported a national wilderness system bill.

When President Johnson signed the Wilderness Act into law in a ceremony in the Rose Garden at the White House on September 3, 1964, it was truly a victory for the environmental movement. The Wilderness Act mandated the creation of a wilderness system selected from federal lands that would be reserved from all forms of development. In part, it was a logical extension of the Echo Park controversy and the sacred-profane distinction of land encoded in the protection of Dinosaur National Monument. The selection of some land as wilderness meant that other lands not chosen for wilderness would be cleared for different uses. At the time, advocates rightly regarded it as a major triumph. The Wilderness Act illustrated the importance of conservation and its still-developing political power. In the cultural climate of the early 1960s, optimistic, visionary, and vaguely utopian, its passage successfully overcame resistance, especially that of many prodevelopment congresspeople, to a piece of legislation that curtailed development.

The passage of the act illustrated the growth of influence of the revitalized and transformed conservation movement as it reflected the affluence and optimism of the United States in the mid-1960s. At the core of the victory were people such as Howard Zahniser, who died of a heart attack just before passage of the bill, and David Brower—individuals who had led the fight for wilderness since the battle over the Echo Park Dam. Out of the remains of the old conservation movement, they had successfully played on the changing value system of the American public, its hopes, fears, aspirations, and challenges, to forge a movement different from the efficiency-based, elitist movement of the early twentieth century. Between Echo Park and the signing of the Wilderness Act, this new movement defined itself and its goals in a manner that the increasingly affluent and expanding middle class could embrace. The result was a movement that tugged at the heartstrings of the most influential portion of the American public, the broad and prosperous middle class of the late 1960s, and that spoke to an important range of its concerns.

THE LIMITS OF SUCCESS

But the battle against the Echo Park Dam and the movement to pass the Wilderness Act failed to expand the range of issues that those who advocated environmental causes addressed. Despite its newfound popularity, "environmentalism," increasingly the label for this revived and transformed conservation movement, was still narrowly confined within American society. Its objectives were oriented toward wilderness and wild places. In most cases, "environmentalists" of the 1950s and early 1960s took little notice of urban sprawl and pollution except in the most peripheral of ways. Environmentalism had expanded the reach of the conservation movement and had created a new and broader constituency for it, but it had not increased the range of issues that concerned its adherents.

Despite such limitations, the period between the early 1950s and the signing of the Wilderness Act in 1964 was a time of great gain for environmental advocates. The affluence of American society, its optimism and faith in the future, allowed both the passage of legislation such as the Wilderness Act, which reserved large areas of potentially economically valuable land, and the idealism characteristic of other Great Society programs. A nation in which standards of living rose every year could afford to set aside a part of its bounty for noneconomic, spiritual, and cultural reasons, and Americans did so with gusto. Their actions forced new management roles onto the agencies charged with administering federal lands.

Chapter 3

INSTITUTIONAL ENVIRONMENTALISM: FEDERAL AGENCIES AND THEIR PUBLICS

The increased interest in environmental issues spawned by the cancellation of the Dinosaur National Monument dam changed the context in which the federal government managed its holdings. All federal agencies that dealt with land or administered development projects, including entities such as the U.S. Army Corps of Engineers, the Forest Service, the National Park Service, the Bureau of Reclamation, and the Bureau of Land Management, had distinct constituencies, large holdings or ongoing management situations, and long-standing patterns of administration. Since the turn of the century, they had relied on conservation groups as allies in the efforts to sell their plans to Congress and the public. But the emergence of a new type of environmental advocacy in the aftermath of the dam controversies of the 1950s had a profound impact on these agencies. Instead of narrow and influential special-interest groups to support their activities, they found a large, contentious, and energized public that subscribed to a different value system. The interest of this broadened public and the often clumsy manner in which federal agencies related their goals and objectives led to a breakdown in relations between the emerging environmental movement and the agencies that managed public land. In this new climate, conservationist and environmental groups spoke for a growing segment of the public and often challenged decisions that earlier organizations and individuals had been willing to support.

The result was a changing matrix of management. Federal agencies ceased to manage on the basis of scientific principle, instead anticipating a trend in American society: they soon learned first to respond to public opinion, to the increased media coverage of environmental issues and the burgeoning interest of an even larger segment of the public, and later to attempt to anticipate the wishes of the public. This kind of preemptory self-censoring led to more convoluted, less rationally based decision-making, a decline in the estimation in which the public held most agencies, attacks on them by their erstwhile supporters, and a general decline in agency morale, sense of mission, and performance. Life in the court of public opinion inexorably changed the way in which federal agencies operated when it came to the American environment.

THE NATIONAL PARK SERVICE

The National Park Service suffered the most tumultuous fall from grace. The Park Service had been created as an agency that appreciated and developed public support. Mather, its first director, made his fortune in the promotion of borax and understood the modern pseudoscience of public relations. Aggressively promoting the agency, he built a broad, powerful, and affluent constituency for the national parks that continued to support the concept into the 1950s. With the help of Rosalie Edge, a longtime park advocate; Robert Sterling Yard, who had been the first president of the National Parks Association; and journalists such as Robert Underwood Johnson at the beginning of the century and later Irving Brandt, the Park Service could count on a vocal and organized constituency to support its programs, supportive and often extensive media coverage, and, as a result, a willing and usually friendly Congress.

Generally, this support system was precisely that: it was ready, awaiting the call of the Park Service, and it usually sprang into action in response to Park Service efforts to mount new programs and increase expenditures. Newspaper editors and influential individuals could be marshaled to contact congressional representatives at a moment's notice. These people were welcome visitors to congressional offices, and federal agencies reciprocated by keeping their constituents informed. This organized campaigning also helped contain independent thinking by supporters. Rarely before the late 1950s did the various private entities that comprised the support system of the Park Service have their own agenda. Even more infrequently did their goals clash with those of the agency.

The Echo Park situation and the subsequent battle for the Wilderness Act began to change the stasis in which Park Service support groups were locked. The forced departure of Newton Drury contributed to a sense that the Park Service could not defend itself, and the sometimes laggard approach of the agency to the question of wilderness raised concerns. Mainstream environmental groups such as the Sierra Club and the Wilderness Society had embraced the idea of a general wilderness bill. Members of these organizations could not help wondering about the Park Service as it dissembled on the leading environmental issue of the day.

Worse for the Park Service was its new position between constituencies. Park Service officials in the parks and in the regional offices became sensitized to the demands of the environmental constituency and began to alter the nature of Park Service attractions. In some cases, such as the termination of the firefall at Yosemite National Park and the "Rock of Ages" ceremony in Carlsbad Caverns—two of many attractions that were unrelated to the features for which the parks had been established but that had been codified by years of practice—agency decisions created controversy and strife. People with long and positive memories of such activities struggled to understand the reasons for their elimination. In other instances, such as the agency's desire to end recreational activities such as skiing within the parks, the changes in policy were insufficient to garner the support of the new environmental movement and simultaneously managed to alienate older supporters—the very constituency for the activities that were terminated. Caught in limbo between its friends and the groups it increasingly sought to cultivate, the Park Service floundered.

There were new influences on federal agencies as well. Changing statutes, new rules and regulations, and additional directives from Congress and other policy-makers changed the Park Service's responsibilities. By the middle of the 1960s, the Park Service experienced a range of new and different factors that affected management. The passage of the Historic Preservation Act of 1966 gave the agency new responsibilities for which it was poorly prepared. The changing cultural climate and demands of constituencies forced the Park Service to regard its urban areas with new respect. These were the places where blue-collar workers, urban ethnics, and minorities, long ignored in the upper-middle-class formulation of conservation, could experience the park system, and urban minorities especially clamored for more attention. In the social climate of the mid- to late 1960s, when cities exploded in summertime riots with a frightening frequency, urban parks became part of the salve that the federal government tried to apply to the gaping wounds of visible inequity in American society.

This broadened the mission of the Park Service. New historical parks were added to the system in an effort to encompass the emergence of previously ignored aspects of the American past. Places that had significance in African American heritage began to be included in the park system; the Frederick Douglass National Historical Site in Washington, D.C., established in September 1962, is one example. Women demanded a place for their history among the sites of the system. The Women's Rights National Historical Park in Seneca Falls, New York, added to the system in December 1980, provided further evidence of the trend of inclusiveness. By the early 1970s Congress began to regard parks in a new manner. California Representative Phillip Burton, who coined the term "park barreling" to describe his efforts, added places of marginal national significance to omnibus bills to obviate the opposition of colleagues to budget expenditures. When Burton learned that a representative in Congress opposed a spending bill, Burton routinely sought an area to be added to the park system within the representative's district. Parks meant the expenditure of federal dollars, more job opportunities, and ongoing federal largesse. Even the most conservative members of Congress were loath to vote against bills that provided economic opportunity in their home districts.

The people who made up the Park Service, many of whom regarded their occupation as a calling, found these new realities hard to understand. The Park Service prided itself on maintaining the crown jewels of the nation, places where Americans could be moved by the awesome natural and human heritage of the nation. Despite the emphasis on outdoor activity that dominated the Wirth years, most of the park-level people in the agency had little desire to run recreational areas. In their estimation, they had trained to administer revered places, not glorified state parks. A crisis of confidence and direction was building within the agency.

The increasing suspicion directed toward the federal government and its activities that became more common in America as the 1960s progressed also damaged the Park Service. It had been one of the most hegemonizing of agencies, offering a message that people in the agency could embrace and to which they gave great credence. The Park Service and its people were decidedly not cynical, eschewing the pose that had become more typical in the United States, and they had a tendency to lean toward idealism. But the values that dominated agency culture had been formed in a different era, and by the 1960s Park Service people sometimes seemed stereotyped as clichéd loyal public servants. Morale declined as the agency responded to outside attacks, lost the support of many of its friends, and faced the redefining of its mission to place a growing primacy on activities to which the existing culture of the agency afforded little status.

Early in the 1970s the Park Service began to lose the direction that it had regained at its highest levels in 1940 with the ascension of Newton Drury to the directorship. Although they differed in philosophy and perspective, Drury and Wirth were leaders in the mold of Mather and Albright—dynamic individuals who brought to the director's position a vision of what the park system could be. Cut from the same cloth was George B. Hartzog Jr., who became director upon Wirth's retirement in 1964. Bold and innovative, such leaders carried the Park Service. But progress was torpedoed in 1972 with the politicization of the director's office. President Richard Nixon fired Hartzog and appointed to the job Ronald Walker, his campaign director and a man with no experience with parks, and a decade-long drift followed through three subsequent directors. By 1980 the result was a demoralized agency.

Much of this could be attributed to the changing nature of American politics, but the agency's inability to respond to the demands of the newly energized public was an equal contributor to the decline of its initiative. Beginning with the perception that the Park Service opposed the Wilderness Act for expedient reasons, the constituency that historically supported the agency began to abandon its slavish fealty to NPS goals. The most dramatic example of this change in attitude was the National Parks Association, which later became the National Parks and Conservation Association. This organization had been established in 1919 by Mather to support the park system; by the 1970s its officials and position papers were often critical of the goals and objectives of the Park Service.

These issues came to a head in numerous situations and circumstances. The establishment of designated wilderness within existing parks after 1964 caused problems for the Park Service and its constituencies as the Park Service dragged its feet while the public clamored for more reserved land. New parks that lacked national significance garnered much local support, but they were criticized by agency activists and their friends in environmental organizations. Questions about the distribution of the Park Service budget emerged. The crown jewels, the old-line national parks such as Yosemite and Yellowstone, had to vie for resources to maintain their declining physical facilities while millions of dollars were spent on new parks of—at least in the old Park Service's estimation—questionable value. Responding to a concerned but sometimes hostile public created a different tenor within the agency.

THE FOREST SERVICE

Other agencies experienced much the same fate. The Forest Service suffered many of the same circumstances as it made the transition from its role managing wartime boom conditions to its new role as the nation's peacetime supplier of timber. Although total timber sales during World War II initially rose and then plateaued at a level far exceeding that of 1939, national forest timber sales increased throughout the war, from 1.5 billion board feet (bbf) in 1941 to 2.8 bbf in 1944 and 2.7 bbf in 1945. The war depleted nonfederal stocks of mature timber, and the postwar housing boom accelerated the already tremendous demand for Forest Service timber. The agency found itself caught between the timber industry, which accused the Forest Service of "hoarding" valuable resources, an increasingly politicized public that was interested in wilderness, and the demands of local constituencies such as ranchers and small timber-cutting operations, long a primary source of agency support. At a time when it needed its best leadership and the strength of its principles, the Forest Service became a weakened agency.

In this context, the Forest Service was susceptible to capture by various portions of its constituencies. Beginning in the immediate postwar period, private timber companies began to cut their own lands at rates that exceeded the natural annual tree growth to meet the demands of the burgeoning construction industry. This led to increasingly strident demands that the Forest Service make available more of its timber for cutting, compelling government foresters to struggle with the gulf between the goals of their agency and the demands of one of their primary publics. The result was a battle within the agency that challenged its very principles.

At the beginning of this battle, conservationists within the Forest Service appeared to be losing. Timber sales on national forest lands increased from 2.5 bbf in 1946 to 4.2 bbf in 1952 and continued to rise. As it had in the age of Pinchot, timber took precedence over all other agency activities, but the 1950s were precisely the moment when the Forest Service way of thinking about the distribution of resources—the idea that federal bureaucrats are better managers than are ordinary businesspeople—fell out of favor. With the advent of the Eisenhower administration, the comprehensive timber cutting that had been common after World War II became sanctioned in policy. Practices such as clearcutting—the indiscriminate cutting of entire stands of trees regardless of species diversity, maturity of the trees, or concerns for habitat—became common. The Forest Service soon found itself cutting more trees with less scientific rationale for its actions while simultaneously grappling with the idea of assisting in better management of privately owned timber land. It was a paradoxical position that pitted agency actions against the principles of its revered founder.

At the same time, the expansion of the national forest system, a consistent factor in agency policy since early in the twentieth century, also ended. The policies of the Eisenhower administration were antithetical even to the addition of national forest land. Eisenhower's was the first twentieth-century administration that did not seek to expand federal holdings, and in fact it actively opposed setting aside additional land for the national forest system. Disputes about the extent of public ownership became important to the Forest Service in a new manner; under the watchful eye of the administration, even exchanges of timber for land, a standard agency practice, were frowned upon. Besieged by industry and without the support of the federal government, the Forest Service had to redefine both its mission and its constituency.

With the ascension of Richard McArdle to the chief forester's position in 1952, the Forest Service had a fresh and flexible leader, but it lacked any means to reconcile conflicting demands on its various lands. Its battles with the timber industry had left the agency unsure of its public support. An awkward decade ensued, during which the agency floundered as it tried to fashion a new ethos that allowed it to meld its heritage with the dreams of a different era. By ending its long-standing habit of castigating the timber industry, the agency lost one thread that sewed its many internal factions together. Instead it found the newly emerging environmentalism, shaped by the Dinosaur National Monument controversy, as its new opponent. In effect, this shift took a perspective that had deep if often peripheral roots in agency culture since its inception and demonized it.

The Forest Service had defined itself through changing times by challenging the goals of the timber industry. Since the 1930s it had actively sought regulation of the privately held timber lands, but the drive for such a goal within the agency died during the early 1950s. At the exact moment when the Forest Service could benefit politically from a stance that advocated the regulation of private timber, it shifted its direction, backing the timber industry and dropping any ties to recreational users and wilderness advocates. This ironic and politically misguided shift to an extreme utilitarian position created the context that put the Forest Service on the defensive as the environmental revolution took place.

As the Forest Service faced increasing opposition to its policies, it shifted back and sought to recapture a middle position. Fearing the advances of other federal agencies, in particular the Park Service and its MISSION 66 program, the Forest Service cast about for a solution. The reshaping of an old idea into a doctrine of "multiple use" became the method that the agency tried to maintain its status and position. This concept, present from the inception of the agency but often ignored in the rush to manage timber, suggested that forested lands could be used in a variety of ways, typically simultaneously. In this concept, recreation, timber-cutting, and other uses could coexist on the vast acreage of publicly owned forested land.

The Forest Service had always paid lip service to the idea of multiple use. Early in the century, the agency had been far more interested in wilderness than had the Park Service, and much of what was exciting in its philosophical evolution came from areas outside of timber management. Its pantheon of heroes—Aldo Leopold, Robert Marshall, and Arthur Carhart, among others—all saw the use of forests in a broad manner. Wilderness and recreation without the amenities that the Park Service provided and that foresters disdained had a place in the cosmology of the agency. But in the actions of the Forest Service, and in its emphasis and direction, timber management dominated all other aspects of national forest management.

The standard bearer for multiple use during the 1950s was Assistant Chief Forester Edward C. Cliff, a veteran of more than two decades in the Forest Service. Although initially lukewarm about the concept, Cliff came to embrace it. He hoped that it would end the pull on the Forest Service from various directions. In his view, the agency served as a referee between various competitive groups of forest users. These users often regarded the Forest Service, not other users, as their adversary, a situation that Cliff hoped to resolve with new multiple-use regulations. "Operation Multiple Use" became Cliff's watchword as he sought to provide more wood for the nation, better hunting and fishing sites, more and higher-quality water, greater outdoor recreation opportunities, and improved range land with better forage.

This "all things to all people" approach belied a more complicated reality. When the Multiple Use-Sustained Yield Act became law on June 12, 1960, it codified a range of practices in law without establishing priorities among them. Timber, wildlife, range, water, and outdoor recreation all became obligations of the Forest Service; each was to be managed by the principle of sustained yield—that is, by the idea that the maximum rate of extraction was that which could be sustained without depleting the resource in question. All categories of resource users had to be served in this formulation but not necessarily in the same geographic place. It was a confusing and sometimes amorphous way to require an agency to make policy, but the Multiple Use-Sustained Yield Act had come from the agency, and the agency would be compelled to live by it and with it.

Multiple Use put the onus of management squarely on an ideologically and culturally weakened Forest Service. Timber had long been its religion, and for a long time timber-cutting and other uses had been able to coexist because none made a significant dent in the vast forested acreage. But the growth in timber consumption and cutting as well as in recreational use in the post-World War II era effectively called the question. Both types of uses increased so dramatically that they began to overlap, even when foresters did not want them to. It was no longer possible to keep recreational users from traveling newly created forest roads to clear-cut areas and other places that offered an unpleasant picture of the practice of timber-cutting. With the growing recreational interests demanding that the commercial cutters be slowed, the Forest Service had to negotiate a way between conflicting constituencies.

Wavering between increasingly powerful constituencies that bounced it between them like a ball, the Forest Service fully felt the impact of public opinion from the conservationist and environmentalist organizations that helped to shape it. The timber industry, a long-standing adversary, scaled up its pressure upon the Forest Service to allow more acreage to be cut; at the same time, the recreational community, growing in size and influence, demanded better facilities and more opportunities while it abhorred the destruction and waste that its members regarded as a part of the legacy of timber-cutting. Instead of a decrease in the pressure on the agency, the pressure and its significance in the decision-making process were amplified.

For foresters, this new reality was something of a shock. The Forest Service had long seen itself as being committed to a democratic ideal of egalitarian management with the best and highest needs of the nation as its guide. Tied to principles developed at the turn of the century, foresters had not adapted well to the post-World War II climate. In the freer-wheeling, more disingenuous post-1945 era—when values became far more malleable and constituencies wavered, responding emotionally to tactical decisions—the Forest Service operated at a disadvantage. With new and different values intruding on the dated ideology of the agency, foresters had to adjust their perspectives, and in fact, their philosophical perspective. The Forest Service had to find a world-view and a set of strategies to allow it to function in the new cultural and political climate.

A new attitude for the agency meant both more flexibility and a broader sense of what was important. In an agency where utilitarian conservation had always been paramount, introducing new values and articulating their primacy remained a difficult project. Three generations of foresters had perceived timber management as the primary and often the sole mission of the Forest Service. Despite the various programs and the public fealty accorded the idea of multiple use in the Forest Service, timber retained its dominant position. As the public began to assert its views regarding national forests in the same manner that it had regarding national parks, and as recreational interests in particular expressed concerns about the management of national forests, the Forest Service soon found its strategies challenged and its actions opposed.

As multiple use became the dominant policy, problems regarding the overlapping of different kinds of uses came to the fore. The appeal of the multiple use doctrine was its raw malleability. Lacking prescribed distinctions between different categories of land use, the Forest Service subtly argued that each piece of land could sustain multiple use. This overlapping patchwork allowed timber to remain the most important use, increasingly to the consternation of supporters of recreation and other uses.

Proposals for a bill to preserve wilderness areas emboldened the environmental community and threatened the Forest Service. As did the Park Service, to manage its areas the Forest Service needed administrative discretion, which any restrictive legislation such as a wilderness bill would curtail. Foresters opposed the various wilderness bills, fostering the notion that federal agencies paid greater attention to the needs of organized commercial interests than those of the general public. But as recreational use increased and logging roads cut deeper into roadless areas, the fear of the public—that the national forests and the Forest Service had been captured by the timber industry—seemed more and more valid.

When the Wilderness Act passed in 1964, foresters took it as a rebuke as much as did their counterparts in agencies such as the Park Service. The passage of the act seemed a repudiation of the concept of multiple use because wilderness in the Forest Service view was conceptually a single-use program. In its statutory definition, it could not coexist with logging, grazing, or even such seemingly less-intrusive uses as recreation or the impoundment of water. Only wildlife preservation and wilderness seemed compatible, and from the point of view of an agency that had hung its future on the idea of multiple use, the bill put disastrous limits on its prerogatives.

The Wilderness Act also squeezed the Forest Service between the timber industry and the new recreation- and wilderness-oriented public. Both took the agency to task for its decisions: advocates of wilderness and recreational use claimed that the Forest Service favored timber operators, and the timber industry claimed that the agency kowtowed to the wilderness community. Caught between its various constituencies, the Forest Service had to find a new middle position that pleased its various "friends." It lacked the ideological tools to accomplish this, wavering from goal to goal. The struggle to accomplish this elusive balancing act defined agency policy as federal agencies came under greater and greater fire. Weakened by its attempts to please everyone, the Forest Service became another of the federal agencies that responded to the most vocal parts of its public and that, like a thin reed in a strong wind, bent whichever direction the wind blew.

THE BUREAU OF LAND MANAGEMENT

The weakest of the federal agencies, the Bureau of Land Management (BLM), also floundered in the new circumstances. Formed in 1946 out of the merger of the old General Land Office and the relatively new Grazing Service, the BLM began with the need to establish an identity distinct from other land-management agencies. It had inherited a broad range of types of land, bound together by the reality that its holdings were comprised of lands that no one had previously claimed and that the government had never designated for any purpose. This hodgepodge was hard to categorize and consequently hard to manage. At a time when the responsibilities of federal agencies seemed to overlap more and more, finding a unique and discrete mission proved to be a difficult task for the BLM. At its founding, the new agency had no new mandate. It only assumed the responsibilities of its predecessors-responsibilities that were hardly close to the mainstream of land-and natural-resource policy. This gave the new agency no clear charter. Blazing a trail that led to permanence and respect for the mission of the agency was a difficult task.

The individual who established a sense of mission for the BLM was an early director, Marion Clawson (1948–1953). Clawson came from Nevada, the son of a ranching family who had gone on to receive a doctorate in economics from Harvard University. When the BLM was formed, he became regional administrator in San Francisco, ascending to the directorship after the departure of Fred H. Johnson, the first director of the new agency. Clawson embodied the kind of visionary spirit that successful bureaucracies must have if they are to survive the vagaries of political fate. Given his mandate by Secretary of the Interior Julius Krug, Clawson set out to transform the new agency.

With the BLM's marginal relationship to the changes in American conservation, Clawson was able to build his bureau in relative quiet. Grazing had been the major obligation of both the agencies that the BLM succeeded, but its lands and programs were not in the forefront of the concerns of 1950s protoenvironmentalism. Only the Sierra Club sometimes challenged the impact of grazing regulations, but during the 1950s the group's resources and much of its energy were tied up in the fights about dams on western rivers. As a result, Clawson could operate out of the view of public opinion, escaping the glare cast by controversies such as the one over the Dinosaur National Monument dam and contending only with hostile entities in Congress.

Clawson began by following the model of the Forest Service and decentralizing the decision-making as well as the functions of the BLM. He arranged to accelerate the permit process for various uses of BLM lands, remarking that "the number and variety of applications for use of the public lands . . . never ceased to amaze me." Clawson happened upon a constituency-the broad array of economic users of public lands-and through his streamlining of the bureau and its procedures, he sought to bring them close to his agency. Even the emblem of the agency that Clawson introduced in 1953, which depicted a miner, a surveyor, a logger, a cowboy, and an oil worker, spoke to the need for a constituency and the desire to create one to serve. Recreational users were conspicuous by their absence in Clawson's new emblem.

The focus on constituency led to charges by scholars that the BLM in particular had been captured by its users. Much of the evidence to support such charges came from the BLM's grazing operation. Since the days of the Grazing Service, advisory boards merely codified local culture and custom concerning range animals. Between 1875 and the passage of the Taylor Grazing Act in 1934, stock concerns had run as many animals as they wanted on public land; the Taylor Grazing Act simply added official sanction to existing practices. Although Clawson sought scientific management of BLM range and limits on grazing, he found that local users had great power and a strong proprietary feeling about federal land. In its desire to develop a constituency, the BLM often catered to local desires, sometimes excluding national interests such as the conservation community.

At the same time, Clawson sought to develop a conservation ethic for his agency, stressing the goals of 1950s conservation in management programs. His programs, which included land classification and inventory, area administration, professionalization of staff, and other innovations, laid the foundation for better management programs on BLM lands. But as a captive of its short history as much as other agencies, the bureau still supported grazing interests above all others.

Clawson accomplished a great deal during his tenure as BLM director, but he was unable to protect his agency from political machinations. Fired by the Eisenhower administration on grounds of insubordination when he refused a request to resign, Clawson departed in 1953. His successors subscribed to Secretary of the Interior Douglas "Giveaway" McKay's philosophy of using federal resources to support business and industry and of giving private users of public land a freer hand. McKay's administration removed the few controls that Clawson was able to implement. Although the McKay philosophy was popular with special interests such as the timber industry and the grazing industry, it rang hollow for the increasingly energetic general public.

Under Edward Woozley, Clawson's successor, most of the work that Clawson initiated was undone. Woozley advocated less federal power and more state autonomy in the decision-making process, attempting to return power to the locals who had held it for so long until Clawson arrived. Woozley was most proud of his ability to generate revenue with the resources of the BLM, and in fact the revenue generated by the bureau rose precipitously during the early years of his administration before returning to lower levels. Much of this increase in revenue came from allowing timber to be cut more widely on BLM land.

Recreation received relatively short shrift under Clawson and Woozley, although for entirely different reasons. Under Clawson, the bureau sought to frame its mission, and its need for a specific, focused constituency required emphasis on commercial users such as the small ranchers whom Clawson believed to be essential to the future of his bureau. BLM lands lacked the appeal of national parks and the scenic and psychic mystique of national forest wilderness. Under Woozley, recreation was largely ignored as the effort to develop marketable commercial resources proceeded at a rapid rate. Timber-cutting and oil and uranium development increased dramatically on federal lands during Woozley's tenure. Even later in the 1950s, when the issue of adequate space for public recreation became an important national issue and recreational uses of public lands dramatically increased, the BLM largely ignored the recreational constituency.

The Kennedy administration brought a new conservation philosophy in 1960, and again the BLM changed course. Kennedy's secretary of the interior, Stewart Udall, an Arizona native who walked a delicate line between development and preservation, fashioned a new conservation agenda for which he requested congressional authorization. Included in it was the reshaping of the BLM's mandate to resemble the multiple-use philosophy of the Forest Service. One result of this reshaping was the Classification and Multiple Use Act (CMU), which compelled the BLM to develop a proactive, comprehensive planning structure for the lands it managed rather than continue in the reactive, case-by-case approach that had been followed. The results were mixed, but the BLM operated with a new measure of flexibility because it could finally take national interests as well as local ones into account as its officials made policy.

Despite attempts to meet a wide range of objectives, the BLM remained a comparatively weak agency. It reacted to all kinds of pressures, from Washington, D.C., down to the local level. The directorship was always politicized, a situation that was a relatively new development for agencies such as the Park Service and the Forest Service. Each new presidential administration fired the sitting director, who represented the goals of the previous administration. There was little continuity in leadership, and a fragmented agency culture developed. At the local level, intransigent officials who had exercised significant power over federal lands resisted any changes that might intrude upon their prerogative. Most of the local boards that BLM set up as it decentralized were not interested in scientific management with its reliance on complicated concepts such as carrying capacity; instead they wanted to run animals on the public range for the cheapest possible cost without regard for the consequences. Unsteady even under Clawson, its most forceful director, the bureau wavered in response to various special interests.

THE BUREAU OF RECLAMATION

Even the Bureau of Reclamation, the most powerful of these agencies at the end of World War II, found itself severely chastened by the changing climate of the 1950s and 1960s. The bureau had made its reputation as an agency with an aggressive posture. It promoted large-scale water-development projects with great success, beginning with the Hoover Dam and continuing through the Colorado River Storage Project. But the battle for Echo Park Dam was the death knell of the public's unwavering support for an ethic that historian Donald Worster has described as "taking pride in pushing rivers around." Bureau of Reclamation projects, always

framed in terms of national funding for local and regional benefit, began to encounter resistance from a swath of the public that
neither resided in the vicinity of projects nor depended on them
for their economic livelihood. These publics, spread across the
nation, saw aesthetic and recreational concerns as having importance equal to that of irrigation, hydroelectric development, and
other more characteristic bureau objectives and justifications as
the number of free-flowing American rivers precipitously
declined.

Accustomed to broad-based currency with state legislatures
and in particular with western congressional delegations, the
bureau barely recognized the need to alter its position. Particularly during the Kennedy and Johnson administrations, when
western congressional representatives controlled the most important capital development-oriented committees, the bureau could
safely relax as its friends on the Hill carried its proposals to
fruition. This created a smugness among agency leadership, a
sense of invincibility that was detrimental to the long-run success
of bureau plans. Secure with its existing power base, the Bureau
of Reclamation simply ignored the changes in public attitudes, a
strategy that exacted an enormous toll on the agency's internal
operations and deeply wounded its public image.

Echo Park challenged the primacy of the Bureau of Reclamation, but knocking its officials off their pedestal required a concerted campaign by a range of activists and public entities. The
Sierra Club played a prominent role in the bureau's fall from public grace. Brower had initiated the club's disenchantment with the
bureau in the late 1940s, a disenchantment that hardened over
the Echo Park controversy. The construction of the Glen Canyon
Dam, which inundated a sizeable portion of land in southern Utah
and regulated the flow of water through the Grand Canyon, awak-
ened the club to the issues of sacred and profane space. The club
had not resisted this dam, deciding to concentrate its energies
on opposing the Echo Park project. By the mid-1960s, it had come
to regret that decision. As officials prepared to close the gates of
Glen Canyon Dam and fill the empty lake behind them, Brower
himself sought to halt the process. Instead he found himself

shunted off to a news conference held by Secretary of the Interior Stewart Udall as the lake began to fill. Disappointed with themselves, the leaders of the Sierra Club prepared to win future battles with the Department of the Interior and its Bureau of Reclamation.

The Sierra Club's overtly political stance was neither entirely new nor particularly foreign. Its leaders had always used connections to power to achieve their ends. What was different about the new setting was the ends to which they sought to devote their energies. Instead of becoming an outlet for the energies of people with faith in progress, the club became a bastion, in fact a magnet, for people who were uncomfortable with the go-go pace of the modern age. This both energized the club and created ongoing contradictions within it.

These impulses came to a head not over the Glen Canyon Dam, but rather over its successors, two dams proposed for the Grand Canyon in the mid-1960s. Brower remained suspicious of even the conservation-oriented Udall, believing the secretary conscientious about places far from his home state of Arizona but dilatory about resisting development in the rest of his native region. Tied to the politics of his arid state, Udall was particularly conscious of water-development issues. The proposal for the two Grand Canyon dams emanated from a project of his, the Pacific Southwest Regional Water Plan, which included comprehensive development of the lower Colorado River. When Arizona planned the Central Arizona Project, a major water-diversion project, in the aftermath of Arizona's victory in the U.S. Supreme Court Arizona v. California Colorado River water allocation case in 1963, conservation advocates within and outside of the Sierra Club felt that Udall betrayed them. The plan and its many ramifications confirmed every suspicion that Brower harbored, energized the environmental movement, and exacerbated the existing problems that the Bureau of Reclamation faced.

The Bureau of Reclamation also failed to fashion a comprehensive strategy to defend itself against attacks on its projects and on its very ethos by Brower and the Sierra Club. By the mid-1960s public sentiment had begun to shift away from the idea of damming rivers, but the commissioner of the Bureau of Reclamation, the immensely powerful and outspoken Floyd Dominy, failed to recognize the shift. Attacking the predictions about the project's ability to generate more usable water, the Sierra Club forced important rethinking by bureau strategists. This kind of attack Dominy could handle, but far more devastating was the public scrutiny that emerged when the Sierra Club took the issue to the public. Full-page advertisements in the Washington Post, New York Times, Los Angeles Times, and San Francisco Chronicle attacked the dams; in response to a Bureau of Reclamation argument that tourists would better appreciate the Grand Canyon from motorboats on the lakes behind the dams, one Sierra Club advertisement responded: "Should we also flood the Sistine Chapel so that tourists can get nearer the ceiling?" Afterward, mail to the bureau ran more than eighty to one against the project.

By 1967 only Dominy and Arizona Congressman Carl Hayden, a veteran of more than fifty years on Capitol Hill and still an important player in water politics, continued to support the idea of dams in the Grand Canyon. Dominy believed that Brower and the conservationists were liars, and he believed that the location of the dam, in the Grand Canyon National Monument, not in the national park itself, proved that his adversaries were disingenuous. But no one was listening, especially to such a dubious distinction about the status of land. Reader's Digest attacked the dams in March 1966, followed by Life magazine. "Then we got plastered by My Weekly Reader," recalled Dan Dreyfus, one of Dominy's most important assistants and, as a New York Jewish intellectual, an anomaly in a bureau made up of westerners and a significant percentage of Mormons. Public sentiment overwhelmingly opposed the Grand Canyon dams, and it was apparent that the Central Arizona Project would never be built with them. In the end, Udall circumvented Dominy, and on September 30, 1968, Lyndon Johnson signed the Colorado River Basin Project Act—including the Central Arizona Project, dams in New Mexico and Utah, and an aqueduct from Lake Mead to Las Vegas—into law. Conspicuous by their absence were the Grand Canyon dams.

With his battle against the Grand Canyon dams, Brower tapped into another reservoir of resentment in modern culture. Progress had become increasingly tainted in American society as a result of the Cold War, and as Vietnam escalated, even that paragon of the Cold War, the military, drew far greater scrutiny than it ever had before. Brower lived that resentment, that questioning of goals, and successfully articulated it at the moment it became part of the common currency of the nation. In the introduction to *The Place No One Knew*, Brower accepted partial responsibility for the drowning of Glen Canyon and argued that modernity, with its pace, abrogated the basic tenets of American democracy. "Progress need not deny to the people their inalienable right to be informed and to choose," he wrote. "In Glen Canyon, the people never knew what the choices were."

With these words, Brower touched a raw nerve in American society. The framing of the issue as the expropriation of choice by the combination of social and institutional structures and the barrage of unsorted information foretold a major issue in U.S. society. By the middle of the 1960s, the world had become, in the phrase of theorist Marshall McLuhan, a "global village," driven by communications systems, and Americans received images from all over the globe. Yet receiving images and having the information to sort them out on more than an emotional basis remained a problem. This theme dragged through the 1960s and beyond as Vietnam, Biafra, the Soviet invasion of Czechoslovakia, and the assassinations of 1968 flashed on the television screen in front of American eyes. All of these provoked response, but the responses were emotional reactions to the images on the screen, not intellectual or even reasoned reactions to the reality of situations.

As his introduction to *The Place No One Knew* reflected, Brower subconsciously and cannily understood this situation. He was able to tug at the heartstrings of Americans. Stewart Udall had promised Americans on three occasions that he understood that the "quiet crisis" in conservation, a phrase Udall himself coined, required more than technological solutions that rested on the precepts of the market economy. His actions regarding dams and development showed Brower and the Sierra Club that

Lyndon Johnson's "credibility gap," the widely held perception that the president did not tell the truth, extended throughout his administration. In *The Place No One Knew,* Brower and the Sierra Club effectively declared war on the conservation policies of Udall and the Johnson administration-ironically the Interior Department and presidency most sympathetic to the precepts of conservation since Harold L. Ickes and Franklin D. Roosevelt in the 1930s and 1940s.

In this kind of battle, the weapons were words and images. The Bureau of Reclamation offered its own volume, *Lake Powell: Jewel of the Colorado,* as a counter to *The Place No One Knew.* In the introduction to the bureau's volume, Stewart Udall praised the agency and the dam, calling the structure an example of the "creation of new beauty to amplify the beauty which is our heritage as well as [the] creation of more places for outdoor recreation." Dominy shaped and organized the book, which championed Glen Canyon Dam as a symbol of Johnson's Great Society and the individualist values of the era of manifest destiny. The dam "tamed a wild river," Dominy wrote, "made it a servant to man's will." In the eyes of the powerful commissioner, it was conquest in the best American tradition.

No better articulation could be found to show the differences between the perspectives of a growing swath of the public and those of the most powerful natural resource development agency of the time. As an outcome of the across-the-board postwar prosperity in the United States, a growing segment of the public, led by the Sierra Club, had learned to question the ethic of progress for its own sake. Instead, a kind of aestheticism and what have since come to be called quality of life issues began to dominate public consciousness. Following the lead of the Johnson administration and the committees headed by western congressmen, the BLM reflected an ethic that regarded conquest and progress as synonymous. This clash of perspectives that shared almost no place of intersection became the ultimate cultural battle of the environment during this time.

As the 1960s continued and the American cultural revolution encouraged new behaviors and mores, the cultural context of the nation dictated that the Bureau of Reclamation was destined to lose this battle. The Sierra Club answered the bureau's response with a new book, *Time and the River Flowing: Grand Canyon*, recognizing that the real objective of the bureau was a dam that could regulate the flow through the Grand Canyon. The new Sierra Club offering illustrated a wild Grand Canyon, alive and changing, a message that appealed to the public and one that the Bureau of Reclamation did not clearly understand.

The selection of mechanized recreation as a response to growing demands for wild rivers and wilderness reflected the bureau's misreading of the tone and tenor of the moment. The rule of hierarchy and concentrated force, to borrow Worster's phrase, ran up against the increasing sense in U.S. society that order is dangerous and that chaos, if inefficient, is often preferable. Basking in a remarkable affluence, Americans willingly perceived the sacrifice of potential economic advantage for the sake of a potential intangible advantage that could loosely be described as a higher quality of life. The aestheticism embodied in that perception placed wild rivers, not their tamed, dammed counterparts, at the pinnacle of recreational experience. Wild rivers embodied the struggle to prove the worth of the individual in a technological society—so intrinsic to the cultural discontent of the 1960s—and the economic advantages of dams seemed inconsequential and, in the affluence of the moment, unnecessary in comparison.

A Changing Cultural Climate

The 1960s also embodied an on-the-edge kind of daring that stemmed from the rise in the importance of youth culture as children of the baby boom, the massive population explosion that began in 1945 and continued in record numbers through 1964, began their transformative march through American history. The challenge, the proof by deed, became intrinsic as young Americans reshaped society, and in the cultural context of the 1960s the wilderness offered a better venue for such proofs of worth than did any mechanized recreational experience. With technology perceived as a wedge between human beings and their soul or true nature, the range of activities that the bureau offered paled when compared with the "true" experience that a vocal segment of the population espoused and that a few even sought.

Added to the growing distrust of government that the handling of the Vietnam War created and that the Watergate scandal made into cultural folklore, the climate of the 1960s and early 1970s spoke strongly against the activities of powerful and weak federal agencies alike. The Bureau of Reclamation, the National Park Service, the U.S. Forest Service, and the Bureau of Land Management all experienced increased scrutiny from the public; at the same time, the public trusted them and their missions less, understood less about what these agencies accomplished or sought to accomplish, and felt less hesitancy about expressing its distaste for the ideas, programs, and actions of federal land-management agencies.

The result was a situation that confused and confounded federal land managers. As they sought to serve a broader constituency, they found that much of the public did not like what they did. In their efforts to please, federal agencies bent in the wind, abdicating mission and the remnants of their principles as they attempted to please loud disgruntled voices. Federal agencies that managed less on the basis of any evident reasoning and more in response to the demands, reasonable and otherwise, of vocal constituencies became typical in Washington, D.C.

As federal agencies fell further and further into this process, the authority with which their decisions were regarded decreased, and the power they held soon followed. By the middle of the 1970s federal land-management agencies were almost entirely reactive. They gave up the initiative in an effort to please their constituency of the moment. The result was the end of mission-based planning and decision-making and the beginning of a new regime in which decisions were determined by which constituency made the loudest noises. The consequence, for both the standing of federal land-management agencies and the condition of federally owned natural and cultural resources, was disastrous.

Chapter 4

—

IDEALISM, UTOPIANISM, AND THE NEWEST BACK-TO-NATURE MOVEMENT: THE 1960S

The American cultural revolution—the upheaval in values, attitudes, and behaviors that became the signature of the late 1960s—shed much less blood than its counterpart in China, but it had enormous consequences for American society. In the wake of the turmoil caused by attacks on traditional ways of acting and thinking, on formal and informal rules about who was who in American society, even the existing beliefs of the mainstream of the nation began to change. By the end of the 1960s Americans had seen the end of most of the taboos that had once been enshrined in law, widespread changes in the meaning of the symbols of their culture, and significant efforts to alter the rules by which the country's society operated. At the time, these changes seemed full of strife; from a historical perspective, they began a process that altered the very basis of life in the United States.

One consequence of this rewriting of the rules of American society was the elevation of the new environmentalism, which was very much in line with the other cultural changes spawned by the confluence of factors that dominated the 1960s. As had occurred during other periods of sociocultural unrest, of spiritual revival and experimentation such as the 1740s and the period between 1815 and 1850, during the 1960s numerous Americans embraced a kind of utopianism. One of the pillars that supported this sentiment was the idea that humanity would be happier in simpler circumstances. Codified in movies such as *Easy Rider*—a cult film about two young motorcycle riders in search of themselves—and acted out by young people who flocked to communes—cooperative communities often located in rural areas—this sentiment led to far broader and much different kinds of concern for the physical world than was seen even during the heyday of conservation in the Progressive era. The political environmentalism spawned by Echo Park and subsequent legislative successes such as the Wilderness Act became only one dimension of a broadened and far more diverse movement.

A NEW SET OF CONCERNS

As Americans challenged the dominant values of their society, some began to see unbridled economic progress in a different light. Concerns for the consequences of human activity were manifest in popular culture and scholarly discourse. These took many forms as a number of different currents challenging conventional wisdom flowed in the United States. Although the vast majority of these critiques of society were political in nature, a number of very important ones spoke to questions of the status, meaning, and condition of the environment.

Instead of the efficiency that so dominated the scientific conservation of the turn of the century, Americans developed a new ethic that emphasized the concerns of an affluent, optimistic society that envisioned no limits to its possibilities. Building on the themes of Lyndon Johnson's "Great Society"—such as the eradication of poverty in America envisioned in the War on Poverty—Americans up and down the economic ladder sought to improve their quality of life. Among the ways they hoped to accomplish this was to make their world safe from chemical hazards and to reduce long-term threats to the globe. At the same time, they developed a heightened appreciation for the aesthetic and recreational qualities of the natural world.

Much of this transformative ethos was couched in the language of the time, a form of discourse that openly flouted norms and challenged the philosophies that long dominated American society. Its emphasis on the quality of human experience was new and reflected a degree of self-importance that the self-denying conservationists of earlier in the century shared but would have found surprising. By the 1960s Americans had become obsessed with individualism, individual rights, and personal entitlement instead of with the sorts of collective rights and personal obligations that the nation's founders envisioned. As environmentalism gathered momentum, it evolved into a form of cultural protest that, alone among such approaches advanced after the beginning of the 1960s, quickly moved to the center of American society. By the end of the decade, addressing the "environmental crisis" had become part of the consensus of mainstream politics.

This transformation began as much social reform in the United States does—with the work of concerned individuals that captured the attention of the public. The 1960s were full of such statements from a range of directions. Three individuals jumped to the front of discourse while one symbolic image reflected the same fundamental concern: the human race needed to assess its actions more carefully before continuing along the paths it had chosen: Rachel Carson's stunning work of nonfiction, *Silent Spring;* Garrett Hardin's "Tragedy of the Commons," a seminal essay about human behavior in the physical world; Paul Ehrlich's *The Population Bomb;* and the television commercial featuring Iron Eyes Cody, an elderly American Indian man, with tears in his eyes as he beheld the littered mess that America had become, all challenged the idea of unbridled economic progress at all costs.

Rachel Carson was, in the words of biographer Linda J. Lear, an "improbable revolutionary." Shy and reserved, Carson had grown up in a bedroom community near Pittsburgh in western Pennsylvania during the 1920s. Influenced by her mother, who read widely and loved the outdoors, Carson learned about the natural world from an early age. She and her mother often walked along the Allegheny River near their home, through woods and wetlands, and across river flats. The young Carson showed a precocious appreciation for the natural world that was developed at the Pennsylvania College for Women. Carson's mother wanted her daughter to be a writer, and the young woman majored in English

President Jimmy Carter is pictured here with Iron Eyes Cody, an American Indian whose appearance in a well known anti-pollution television commercial symbolized the response to pollution.

for her first two years at school. At the end of her sophomore year, she made a remarkable decision to change her major to biology; this made her one of the elect company of three who comprised that major at her school. When she graduated with distinction in 1929, Carson received a fellowship to the Woods Hole Marine Biological Laboratory in Massachusetts. She followed that by accepting a small stipend to Johns Hopkins University in Baltimore, where she completed an M.A. in zoology in 1932. Although she would have liked to pursue a doctorate beyond the first two courses she was able to complete, the combination of the Depression of the 1930s and her impecunious family situation prevented her from following this dream to fruition.

In 1935 Carson entered the federal service after her father's sudden death made her the primary breadwinner of her family.

She found a part-time job in the Bureau of Fisheries, an arm of the Department of Commerce, where she wrote the scripts for a radio series entitled "Romance under the Water." After she recorded the highest score in the nation on the civil service examination, she received a permanent federal position as a junior aquatic biologist in the Fish and Wildlife Service of the Department of the Interior. Thirteen years later, after having proved time and again her ability to explain science in graceful and clear writing that the public could easily understand, Carson was appointed editor-in-chief of all Department of the Interior publications.

In her free time, Carson pursued a private writing career. She first published in the *Atlantic Monthly Magazine* in 1937, and her first book, *Under the Sea-Wind,* debuted to public acclaim in 1941. Her second book, *The Sea Around Us,* was serialized in *New Yorker Magazine,* became available in 1951, and was an instant publishing success. It remained on the *New York Times* best-sellers list for a number of months and was a primary selection of the Book of the Month Club. The success of the book provided her with sufficient funds to retire from government service to pursue a career as a full-time writer. Other books followed as she engaged in the writing that she found most exciting.

Since her arrival in the Department of the Interior almost twenty years before, Carson had been concerned with the application of synthetic pesticides to crops, rangelands, and other habitat. World War II was a watershed in the development of synthetic chemicals. Organic materials commonly used for control of noxious plants were replaced with inorganic compounds such as DDT (dichloro-diphenyl-trichloro-ethane), a potent chlorinated-hydrocarbon insecticide first synthesized in 1943. Another major type of new pesticide, phosphorous insecticides such as malathion and parathion, also became popular. By 1947 the United States produced more than 125 million pounds of such widely used compounds each year, and the rates of production and use continued to skyrocket. Traces of these new chemicals became pervasive in almost every analysis of the condition of the environment. By the mid-1950s, when Carson received a letter from her friend Olga Owens Huckins that crystallized her nagging concerns, the consequences of the widespread use of synthetics had become apparent. One obvious result, the disappearance of songbirds about which Huckins complained, captured Carson's attention and then that of the nation. The title of her book, *Silent Spring,* succinctly expressed her fear.

Carson was reclusive, but the serialization of *Silent Spring* in *The New Yorker* in 1962 made her a celebrity and created a national sensation. Indicting the chemical industry, agribusiness, and the federal government for the indiscriminate use of chemicals, the published excerpts from the book inspired tumultuous response from every corner of the "respectable" world of industry science. *Time* magazine accused Carson of an "emotional and inaccurate outburst" in an article about her book, and she was criticized by Ezra Taft Benson, formerly secretary of agriculture and later president of the Church of Jesus Christ of Latter-Day Saints. Carson's status as an unmarried woman provoked some fire, while others such as Benson dismissed her in the categorical terms of the time as a "hysterical female."

By the time the book debuted in September 1962, two camps that opposed her work had solidified. One, comprised of Department of Agriculture officials, agribusiness, and the chemical industry, saw the book as a public relations problem, albeit a nightmarish and expensive one. The other camp, the members of the professional science community, regarded Carson's work as a challenge to their integrity. What Carson condemned as a "Neanderthal age of biology" was the dominant paradigm in insect control, the source of the income of many industry scientists, the funding of their research, the significance of their profession, and, for many, their self-esteem.

Carson had touched a raw nerve in American society. She presented only the case against synthetic pesticides instead of also weighing their advantages, but that formulation spoke to a range of concerned citizens across the nation. President John F. Kennedy pledged an investigation of the charges that Carson's work contained even before the book was available in stores and directed

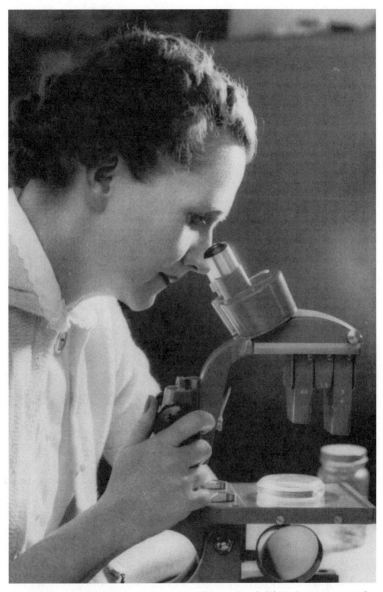

Rachel Carson, a biologist whose non-fiction book Silent Spring *created a national sensation and challenged the idea of unbridled economic progress at all costs.*

his science advisor to set up a committee to look into the questions she raised. When *Silent Spring* debuted, it was an instant best-seller, with more than six hundred thousand copies in circulation the first year. Despite a letter-writing campaign designed to discourage the program, the following spring CBS aired a prime time special entitled *The Silent Spring of Rachel Carson.* The toxicity of progress had become a national issue.

Carson's axiom that "we know not what harm we face" spoke to an important legacy of technological innovation in American society. When the United States used the atomic bomb against Japan at the end of World War II, the American public and even the scientific community responsible for it reacted with a combination of awe, fear, and horror. The atomic bomb was an exceptional device, but the more that people thought about its implications, the less comfortable with it they became. Individuals as diverse as J. Robert Oppenheimer, who directed the Los Alamos project that developed the bomb, statesman John Foster Dulles, and imprisoned Nazi war criminal Hermann Göring all expressed reservations about its use.

The atomic bomb shocked Americans and the world, ushering in a new age and requiring a kind of reflection about the nature of warfare that previously was unnecessary. The image of progress acquired a tarnish that it never entirely lost and that was obscured during the dark days of the Cold War during the 1950s, when national security became paramount. Yet the concern remained in American society, hidden behind the conformity that marked the 1950s. Rachel Carson's presentation of the invisible consequences of pesticide use spoke strongly to suppressed fears in American society.

In 1968 biologist Paul Ehrlich added to the cacophony with a book entitled *The Population Bomb.* Building on an argument about the rate of population growth compared with that of the expansion of food production first offered in 1798 by English philosopher and cleric Thomas Malthus, Ehrlich pointed out that humanity was on a course to self-destruction as a result of the sheer weight of its natural increase. In the most famous section of the book, he described how he came to understand this point "emotionally one stinking hot night in Delhi," India. In the heat of more than one hundred degrees, amidst the smoke and the dust, Ehrlich wrote, "the streets seemed alive with people. People eating, people washing, people sleeping. People visiting, arguing, and screaming. People thrusting their hands through [our] taxi window, begging. People defecating and urinating. People clinging to buses. People herding animals. People, people, people, people." Believing that ever since that night he had known the feel of overpopulation, Ehrlich sought to alert Americans to the inherent problems of the exponential population growth of the modern world.

Another sensation, *The Population Bomb* sold more than three million copies and kicked off an immense debate about the virtues of having more people on the planet. Criticized as a prophet of gloom and doom, Ehrlich initiated a debate that crossed cultural and religious boundaries, affected social policy, and pointed out the inherent problems associated with unbridled technological advance. He showed that sixty Indian babies born the night of his visit to Delhi would consume as much as one American baby who entered the world at the same time. This raised the question of the equity of resource distribution, as well as the problems inherent as the human race engineered solutions to problems of infant mortality, disease, poor crop production, and other maladies that had long affected the species.

Ehrlich's position challenged the reigning views of the Roman Catholic church as well as those of everyone who believed in programs such as the Green Revolution, which transferred American seeds, technology, and pesticides to the people of the Third World in an effort to help them produce crops for market. Church doctrine in the 1960s opposed any form of contraception, but methods of birth control—the most revolutionary of which was the birth control pill, first made available in 1960— had become common in the Western world. Americans remained notoriously laggard in considering the implications of their own population growth, preferring to regard overpopulation as a function of poverty rather than of resource consumption. Americans could afford babies, many seemed to be saying; it was the rest of the world that could not.

The Green Revolution—the package of innovations in practice and the technologies to implement them that were designed to increase commercial agriculture production in the underdeveloped portions of the globe—seemed to offer a way to give the rest of the world that capability. Initiated after World War II, the Green Revolution was designed to bring Third World countries into the global economy by providing them with marketable commodities. Typically the implementation of Green Revolution programs promulgated hybridized seeds that responded to the new classes of synthetic fertilizers, farm management practices based on the use of biocides, and agricultural equipment and machinery to support both extensive and intensive expansion of farming. Often, these programs involved both new irrigation developments and expansion of rain-fed agriculture. In some ways, the process worked. By the late 1960s agriculture had begun to take on market characteristics in many places around the globe.

Mexico offered a prime example. Between 1940 and 1965 agricultural output in Mexico increased by a multiple of four. As a result, that country grew enough to feed its burgeoning population and became a net exporter of food for the first time in its history. Mexican agriculture became a model for the Rockefeller Foundation, the U.S. Agency for International Development, the World Bank, and the other institutions that funded technological advance and economic development in the Third World. Agricultural technology seemed to offer the solution to the predicament of the human race.

But the triumph of the Green Revolution was short-lived. By the 1970s the advances had reversed. Mexico became a net importer of food, and its agriculture was widely perceived as being in a state of crisis. Crops with great market value, particularly specialty fruits and vegetables such as strawberries, asparagus, and broccoli, began to replace staples such as grains and beans in the fields of Mexico. The result was agriculture directed at the international market instead of at food production for home, with disastrous consequences for the multitude of Mexico's poor. The imported staples necessary to feed the population were more expensive than home-grown crops, taking a terrible toll on the impoverished.

Because the Green Revolution had been directed at market agriculture, subsistence production had not undergone a similar revolution. Agricultural land belonged to the wealthy in Mexico, and subsistence production was not sufficient to fill the gap. The poor became poorer and began to move in large numbers, first to Mexican cities and later across the border, often as illegal aliens into the United States. The rich in Mexico maintained control of the land and its wealth, benefitting economically from the burgeoning market in specialty crops.

The results of the Green Revolution confirmed the axioms of another major environmental thinker of the 1960s, biologist Garrett Hardin. In 1968, in a presidential address to the Pacific Division of the American Association for the Advancement of Science entitled "The Tragedy of the Commons," Hardin articulated an idea that has remained revolutionary in U.S. society: that there are classes of problems to which no technical solution exists. As a result, he suggested, Americans needed to reexamine their individual freedoms to see which ones are defensible in light of burgeoning social needs.

To illustrate this point, Hardin demonstrated the problems of societies with shared common resources. Individuals maximize their use of common resources, he argued, saving their own until the common resources are depleted. There was only one Yosemite Valley, to which at the time everyone had access at any time; this openness led to an erosion of the values that most sought within the park—a feeling that is familiar to almost all who have thought that they had a beautiful place to themselves only to hear the voices of approaching strangers. Common areas, he argued, are justified only where populations are not dense. They function well as long as population remains in a static condition, but as soon as substantial growth occurs, for whatever reason, the protection of the commons dissipates. In the thickly populated modern world, Hardin insisted, people need to make more rules to govern their activities. Greater freedom for all would result from this sacrifice of individual liberty.

In many ways this argument ran counter not only to the trends of the 1960s, but also to the idea of freedom as Americans had come to understand it. Hardin had been concerned with the right to reproduce, arguing that "mutual coercion, mutually agreed upon," is the best way to solve the problems of population and, by extension, those of the physical environment at large. In effect, he argued for an earlier, somewhat archaic definition of freedom as collective rights with personal obligations.

ENVIRONMENTALISM AND CULTURAL CURRENTS

But the cultural currents of the 1960s flowed toward individual freedoms; it was during the second half of the twentieth century that the right to do what one pleased—wherever, whenever, however, and with whomever—came to be considered a basic American and even human right. Student protests and alternative cultural expressions had much to with individualism. The famed expression of 1960s angst, "do your own thing," clearly reflected the primacy of the individual. At a time when large numbers of Americans began to express distrust for their government, Hardin advocated commonly agreed-upon solutions in the form of rules and laws—in other words, government—to solve the social problems stemming from overpopulation. As did much else during the 1960s, the problems and the best solutions for them seemed paradoxically and diametrically opposed.

Observing the 1960s in the United States, it would have been hard to predict success for Hardin's strategy. He was a biologist, thinking in the empirical terms of science and arguing for common solutions implemented by government at a time when such solutions to social ills seemed anachronistic at best and more likely misguided. The great outpouring of "antiestablishment" thinking and the destruction of old social, racial, and cultural barriers foretold a more open rather than a more restrictive world. Figuratively freed from their psychic chains, Americans sought more for themselves. Defined in different ways, this thinking permeated the nation and made pleas such as Hardin's heard only in selective quarters.

Despite its obviously politically liberal position, Hardin's formulation became classed as politically conservative. It argued for restrictions when student radicals and the musicians and popular culture heroes who carried their message wanted to, in the words of the Jefferson Airplane song, "tear down the walls." The experimental back-to-nature movement, comprised of people who fled the counterculture of urban streets for seemingly bucolic and idyllic life in rural communes where they would raise their own animals and grow their own food, threw over social norms. Singing songs that preached freedom from social constraints, its members were hardly prepared to submit to government approval before having children.

In fact, they sometimes advocated precisely the opposite. The popular counterculture-based musical group Jefferson Starship, a spin-off of Jefferson Airplane, articulated this premise in a song about the birth of a baby entitled "A Child Is Coming": "What are we going to do when Uncle Samuel comes around, asking for the young one's name? Looking for the print of his hand for his file in their numbers game. I don't want his chances for freedom ever to be that slim." The song continued: "Let's not tell them about him." This sense of freedom as the liberation from restraint of the individual ran directly counter to the ideas of thinkers such as Hardin.

A segment of the young also experimented with communal rural living, mostly without long-term success. Communes were generally populated with young people who had been raised in suburbs, most of whom knew little if anything about agriculture or animal husbandry, the basics of rural life. Occasionally such communes survived, usually by the skill and ingenuity of a dominant leader and the discovery of a specific product to market rather than by the development of a subsistence economy, but most failed, some dismally. In their wake, they left disillusioned and sometimes devastated individuals who, lacking the skills necessary for the life they had chosen, found their idyllic sense of rural life dashed by the harsh reality and sometimes fundamental poverty of their rural experience. Even the communes that survived for a significant time, such as the Taos Commune outside of Taos, New Mexico, experienced constant turnover. The back-to-nature mythology of the 1960s ran hard against the fundamental day-to-day grind of machinery-based and borrowed-capital rural life.

Yet such experimentation reflected a changing value system throughout the nation, a reappraisal of the virtues and vices of American society as it approached the two hundredth anniversary of the signing of the Declaration of Independence in 1976. Despite the transformation of the nation into a world economic power, the development of a massive physical plant and infrastructure to support industrial society, and many other changes, the American universe had yet to be perfected. Before that utopian goal, expressed so widely during the 1960s, could be attained or even approached, there was much to do.

ENVIRONMENTALISM AS A CENTER IN A FRAGMENTED SOCIETY

Out of the uproar in American society environmentalism emerged as something of a compromise position, a place where the construction of a new American society could begin. This position resulted from the long-standing bipartisan consensus in Congress about conservation, which in the polarized 1960s seemed closer to environmentalism than ordinary politics seemed to any other aspect of the new construction of reality in American society. Beginning with the "Keep America Beautiful" campaign, in which First Lady Claudia A. "Lady Bird" Johnson played an instrumental role, and encompassing measures such as the passage of state bills that required deposits on beverage bottles sold within their boundaries, environmentalism captured the public's attention.

Lady Bird Johnson's effort reflected both her personal love of the outdoors and her and her husband's close ties to the land. The Johnsons were both from small towns in Texas, and the president's family had deep if not always successful roots in agriculture and ranching. Both of the Johnsons strongly felt their rural roots, and Lady Bird Johnson in particular felt concerned about the increasingly littered American landscape. Her role as first lady in the 1960s did not allow avenues to make policy, but it did cede to her the traditional sphere of first ladies: issues of social and moral uplift. In this sphere, Lady Bird Johnson became a primary advocate of a number of aspects of the new environmentalism. One aspect that particularly concerned her was the condition of U.S. highways. In 1958 Congress had passed a bill regulating billboards along highways, but its implementation proved unsuccessful. Beginning in 1964 the Johnson administration worked hard to pass a bill that limited billboards on highways in rural areas, although no restrictions were included for commercial and industrial areas. In this, Lady Bird Johnson's interest was evident; after his election in November 1964, Lyndon Johnson called Secretary of Commerce Luther Hodges and said: "Lady Bird wants to know what you are going to do about all those junkyards along the highways." Because of the power of forces in favor of highway billboards, Johnson resorted to the kind of arm-twisting and coalition-building for which he was famous. In the end, the efforts paid dividends. The Highway Beautification Bill passed Congress on October 7, 1965, and was soon signed into law.

Lady Bird Johnson's efforts also included programs to beautify urban areas. Inspired by Stewart Udall, secretary of the interior under presidents Kennedy and Johnson, and by Jane Jacobs, a well-known author and critic of city planning, the first lady began a program to beautify Washington, D.C. Early in 1965 she formed a committee of twenty private citizens that came to be called the First Lady's Committee for a More Beautiful National Capital. Among its members were Udall, philanthropist Laurance S. Rockefeller, Katherine Graham, publisher of the *Washington Post,* and philanthropist Mary Lasker. By April 1966 four hundred thousand bulbs had been planted in parks, public squares, and the triangles that dotted the metropolitan area. Within two years, a full-scale local beautification program had become a fixture in the nation's capital.

There was another dimension of the beautification program that tied into the social programs of the Johnson administration. A portion of the program developed a beautification strategy for inner-city neighborhoods and schools—an aspect that Lady Bird

Johnson enthusiastically supported. She participated in a planting ceremony at the Greenleaf Gardens public housing project in Washington, D.C., in March 1965 and continued to make similar appearances throughout the remainder of her husband's term. Her committee also underwrote two other major programs directed at disadvantaged neighborhoods: Project Pride, which targeted such neighborhoods for cleanup, and Project Trail Blazers, which turned abandoned structures and areas into museums and play spaces for children.

Lady Bird Johnson became the symbol of the beautification movement. She had considerable influence over her husband, and he was a powerful and persuasive president until Vietnam destroyed his credibility. Interviewed in *U.S. News & World Report* about beautification projects, Lady Bird Johnson also became a visible spokesperson, undertaking tours of the country to promote beautification. In 1965 alone she traveled to Virginia, Jackson, Wyoming, Milwaukee, Wisconsin, and Buffalo, New York, on separate beautification trips. This activity continued throughout the presidency and remained an ongoing passion during the retirement that followed. It was easily the most important public effort in which she engaged as first lady, and it was the only one that subjected her to the kind of criticism reserved for political leaders and others who exercise power.

The activities of Lady Bird Johnson helped attract wider attention and constituency for the environmental movement. Poised and gracious, she made a fine symbol in a time of turmoil, and many people gravitated to beautification because Lady Bird Johnson thought it important. The result was a program that had as many symbolic as actual ramifications; it made the environment a more important social issue and identified it closely with mainstream politics.

Another factor in the increased importance of the environment as an issue was the rise in consciousness about pollution. A historic problem, pollution seemed ubiquitous in the late 1960s. Cities such as Los Angeles began to experience "smog"—an amalgam of the words *smoke* and *fog*—resulting from the combination of industrial emissions, automobile exhaust, haze, and other

Los Angelinos responded to smog using the tactics of the 1960s.

pollution that blemished the vistas of cities and made breathing difficult. Litter was everywhere, smokestacks belched, and buildings in many cities were covered with layers of grime. The five Great Lakes, together the largest body of fresh water in the world, seemed polluted beyond comprehension. Much of this resulted from the heavy industrialization along its shores. The Cuyahoga River in Cleveland caught fire on separate occasions before, during, and after World War II because it was so polluted. When the river caught fire again in 1969, it seemed a direct challenge to the ethic of progress. Industrial development had great advantages, but by the end of the 1960s, the cost appeared very high.

Another cause of widespread pollution was the postwar development of synthetic detergents—new types of cleansing agents that created immense amounts of foam that did not dissolve in water, or in the parlance of the day, that were not biodegradable. Suds that filled aeration pools at sewage plants followed, and by late in 1947 sewage plant operators across the United States reported unprecedented foaming. Rivers and lakes throughout America, often sources of local drinking water, soon became polluted as well. As early as 1950, a plant operator of the activated sludge plant in Bartlesville, Oklahoma, had come to see foam as part of his daily operating conditions. "On a good day," he wrote, "the suds sail around in the air like little clouds."

One of the hallmarks of the decade was the battle over biodegradable detergents and the quest to find the solution to this unforeseen consequence of technological innovation. Although usually hidden from the sight of the public, the problem of foaming soaps was soon severe enough to require government regulation. By the middle of the 1950s efforts began to limit the uses of this class of detergents, but success was a long and involved political process that required circumventing the lobbyists of a powerful industry. In 1965 Congress passed bills that limited the importation and manufacture of synthetic detergents while monitoring the response of the soap industry. Over a period of years, the use of foaming soaps was phased out, and by the mid-1970s nonfoaming linear alkyl sulfonate (LAS) detergents became the norm.

The detergent question was a challenge to American norms. By the 1960s Americans had become accustomed to newer and better versions of every household necessity as a way of life; "new and improved" was already a cliché of American life. The challenge to synthetic detergents was a couched attack on the idea that things always could be made better without consequences. It also suggested that the consumption-oriented lifestyle of American society might have flaws. But detergents were a standard commodity in everyday life. When changes in the product ended foaming problems, the larger issue of the relationship between technology and convenience was obviated. The battle over detergents ultimately had only limited resonance. Making pollution a *cause celebré* required a different setting than the laundry rooms and sewage plants of the nation.

THE SANTA BARBARA OIL SPILL

The 1969 Santa Barbara oil spill crystallized pollution problems for the American public. The Santa Barbara coast and its channel were among the most beautiful natural places in North America. The affluent university town that descended from a Spanish pueblo and a 1920s resort for the super rich was a lovely place, full of new ideas and seemingly divorced from the turmoil of the time. On January 28, 1969, a blowout of an oil-well platform off the coast of this unusual town shattered the illusions of insulation that Santa Barbara residents had harbored. The blowout fouled the coast with 235,000 gallons of crude oil, blackening thirty miles of white sand beach. The spill was inescapable in Santa Barbara; it established a direct relationship between pollution and the privileged segments of the American public, the affluent and normally apathetic Santa Barbarans.

The position of Santa Barbara as a place insulated from the worst aspects of American life, as a refuge of the social and economic elite, ironically made it an ideal symbol for the antipollution revolution taking place in American society. When pollution was confined to the vicinity of industrial plants or to neighborhoods filled with blue-collar workers of every European ethnic stripe or of African American and other minority heritage, it was difficult to protest too greatly about the consequences to the places that provided economic sustenance to the community. People recognized that their prosperity entailed risk. At the turn of the century, farmers downwind from smelters encountered resistance if they sought to sue for damages to crops and stock under existing nuisance laws. As early as the 1920s industrial towns experienced disproportionately high numbers of specific ailments; some towns were known for ailments such as "phossy jaw," a result of the white phosphorus used in match factories, while others were known for the rheumatism and arthritis common among stockyard workers. In such cities as Pittsburgh,

Cleanup efforts after the Santa Barbara oil spill, 1969. This disaster captured national attention because it showed that everyone, not only poor urbanites, could be effected by pollution.

Pennsylvania, and Gary, Indiana, the pall that hung over the town was considered part of the cost of enjoying the relative affluence of the industrial middle class. But for Santa Barbara residents, luxuriating in their seemingly idyllic paradise with the wealth that no small number had wrung from the haze that enveloped most industrial communities, the juxtaposition of pollution and their self-proclaimed pure lifestyle meant serious upheavals.

Santa Barbara captured national attention because the spill there threatened the myth of the California dream so central to post-World War II American society. Its residents were who Americans wanted to be, their city the circumstances and location in which Americans aspired to live. Such places had seemed immune to the problems of the modern world prior to the spill, and the fouling of such a place with an essential product for modern life caught national attention. It also helped that the residents of Santa

Barbara were influential enough to make their plight part of national consciousness.

There was a certain hypocrisy to the way in which those who lived in Santa Barbara presented their defense of their homes. Famed mystery writer and local resident Ross MacDonald called the oil spill "an ecological crime—a crime without criminals but with many victims," failing to note that in the terms of international pollution, the Santa Barbara spill was one of many in 1969, and not a particularly severe one at that. Roderick F. Nash—University of California at Santa Barbara historian and author of *Wilderness and the American Mind,* one of the seminal works in American environmental history—read the "Santa Barbara Declaration of Environmental Rights" on national television on the first anniversary of the spill. This new "declaration of *inter*dependence," as Nash put it in the foreword of the text, summarized the problems as people in Santa Barbara saw them and proposed solutions that reflected the idealism of the time. Nowhere did Nash or MacDonald note the culpability of the people who lived in Santa Barbara and who consumed the abundance of America— who drove automobiles that would have used the gasoline made from the crude oil spilled in their channel—in the predicament that they had helped create. In MacDonald's construction, they were passive victims of this misfortune as opposed to active, if indirect, participants in creating the forces that caused it.

The response to the Santa Barbara oil spill illustrated the trap that caught 1960s environmentalism. Only when the problems reached the lives of the privileged did the problems truly attract national attention. The bad air, the poor conditions in factories and plants, and the consequences of working with toxic materials were common and accepted. Since the turn of the century, the nation had recognized that some occupations were more dangerous than others. The result was that those jobs were relatively well compensated compared with similar work to account for the danger involved. In the thinking of the era prior to the 1960s, people had a choice. They were paid for the danger, and they could accept it or find a less-dangerous and presumably lower-paying job.

Although the problems were clear enough to see when they reached someone's backyard, genuine solutions were more difficult. It was easy to fall back on the oppositional rhetoric of the 1960s, to point out the flaws in the "system" rather than to work to find answers to problems that in essence paired risk and prosperity in the most awkward of relationships. Despite calls from Nash and others to give up the comforts of technological civilization for the simple life, Americans were not prepared to give up the amenities of their society and their opulent ways of life to assure a pristine environment. Instead, they wanted to have their figurative cake and eat it, too: they wanted a clean environment and an ever-increasing standard of living. It was not within the realm of public policy to conjure up a way around this most basic of American predicaments.

The Santa Barbara oil spill had other important consequences. It accelerated the move to regard questions of pollution as serious public policy issues in the United States and helped bring the environmental movement closer to the American mainstream. Pollution had increasingly moved to the forefront of the agenda of politicians as the optimistic American population saw the perfectibility of its society within its reach. In an era of increasing emphasis on individual freedom that ironically still regarded government regulation as the solution to social and environmental problems, pollution became something to legislate. The first federal Clean Air Act was passed in 1963; individual states, particularly Minnesota, Wisconsin, and Oregon, began to implement their own antipollution strategies, and a number of national political leaders weighed in on the subject, but the idea remained far from the mainstream. The high profile of the Santa Barbara spill and the realization that anyone any place could in an instant experience the same sort of problem accelerated interest in environmental issues. What had been a dirty secret of American prosperity came out into the open at a time when Americans felt that their institutions needed reevaluation.

In effect, Americans ignored the sanctimonious pronouncements of Santa Barbara residents about their rights and focused on the real issue: pollution, either because of a disaster or because of constant endemic conditions, was a threat to the quality of life that Americans valued. As was disease, pollution was a symptom that could be addressed by devising new systems, and many wanted their laws and their best minds to solve it. Despite Hardin's prescient observation that there are classes of problems that technology can not solve, Americans fell back on their time-honored remedy: concocting a new technology. When this remedy yielded no immediate results, they began to consider new ways of thinking about their use of the natural world.

ENTERING MAINSTREAM POLITICS

In this fashion, the environment entered mainstream American politics. It entered not because of any great enlightenment on the part of Americans, but because of the affluence and privilege at the core of middle-class post-World War II experience. Considering themselves members of a society about to solve its most difficult problems, Americans simply added this one to the mix. The transition was abrupt; as late as 1968 the Brookings Institution did not list ecology among the issues that its members believed that the new Nixon administration should immediately address. Almost overnight, pollution and the environment became issues of national gravity and proportion. With the support of senators such as Gaylord A. Nelson of Wisconsin, environmental issues became central to the political process.

Mass media played an important role in this process. Iron Eyes Cody, the American Indian dressed in a headdress with a tear rolling down his cheek in the famous antilitter TV public service announcements of the late 1960s and early 1970s, played on every American stereotype about the simple life and Native Americans to make a searing point about the American patrimony. Despite the efforts of Lady Bird Johnson, the American landscape was not as beautiful as it had once been. Its shores were covered with broken glass, its highways littered with food wrappers and bottles. The symbolism of the man dressed as a mythic Indian chief conveyed many things: the passing of obligation from the so-called first ecologists to modern people, who had clearly abdicated their responsibility, the reverence in which Americans in general were beginning to regard the Native American past, and the simply disastrous condition of the American landscape. The appropriation of this symbol played an important role in bringing environmental issues closer to the mainstream.

Other iconographic characterizations helped the transformation to mainstream status. The green ecology symbol typified popular culture's response. Public symbolism played an important role in the 1960s, and many people literally wore their beliefs on their sleeves. The peace sign was only the most familiar of such icons. The ecology sign, made popular at the end of the decade, reflected the rise of individual interest in environmentalism as it presented a public affirmation of its importance.

In part, this resulted from the increased activism of a wide swath of the public. By the end of the 1960s Americans had become accustomed to direct action as a way to further their goals. The success of the civil rights movement had taught at least that much. With the encroachment of pollution and environmental degradation into every aspect of life, the rallying cry—that progress must be tempered with a new ethic of responsibility based on consideration of the impact on future generations—was easy for people of various backgrounds and political persuasions to accept. Grass-roots activism and a few sympathetic members of Congress led to a groundswell of support for the expanding environmental movement. Typically, Congress followed the lead of its constituents, and the desires of the environmental community began to be translated into law and policy.

But it would be hard to construe the environmentalism that gained shape and gathered momentum during the 1960s as of a piece with the other political and cultural changes that took place during the decade. Although efforts to extend civil rights shared with environmentalism dependence on government as a means to implement change, environmentalism had more to do with preserving gains than with making them accessible across a wider portion of the population. Of all the suggestions and protests of the 1960s, environmentalism was the one that most easily found a place in the mainstream. In this context, the problems of pollution in particular reflected universal concerns, whereas the more charged political goals of the decade were closely linked only to segments of society. Even the so-called Silent Majority could embrace the call to clean up water and air while keeping its distance from the noise of political change.

As a result, environmentalism became coopted, but in the process its advocates were able to achieve a range of goals that would have been entirely impossible from the outside. Instead of becoming oppositional in the manner of the leftist politics of the decade, environmentalism became a point of healing in the culture wars that racked the United States. When a young radical cleric, Richard Neuhaus, complained in the late 1960s that environmentalism was a "seductive diversion from the political task of our time," he recognized a crucial feature of the new movement. Its beneficiaries were the middle class, already privileged by the standards of revolutionaries, many of whom were the children of the very middle class they sought to fracture. Here generational conflict, so crucial to the 1960s, was muted; here young and old could agree on a set of goals for American society, if not always on the means to attain them. In that narrow center, environmentalism, of all the changes of the 1960s, was second only to the transformation of the concept of individual and group rights in the way in which it transformed American thinking and action. Unlike radical politics, which withered as American involvement in Vietnam slowed and ended in an excruciatingly painful manner, environmentalism gained and retained a political and cultural resonance. As the 1970s began, environmentalists and their supporters had many reasons for optimism.

Chapter 5

ENVIRONMENT REACHES THE GOVERNMENT: NEPA, EPA, EARTH DAY, AND THE REBIRTH OF BIPARTISAN POLITICAL SUPPORT

Perhaps no meteorological event ever had quite the impact on public policy as did the mass of noxious air over Birmingham, Alabama, in November 1971. Although there had been numerous similar instances of air pollution in American history, most notably the killer smog in Danora, Pennsylvania, in 1948, no other incident so clearly reflected the changing values and policies of American society concerning environmental quality. Much of the federal legislation designed to assure better environmental conditions was already in place, but the response to the events in Birmingham became the litmus test for a new ethic. The public and legal reaction, which included the issuing of a court order that limited production by more than 60 percent at the twenty-three largest industrial companies in Birmingham, ushered in what has been called the "environmental decade."

During the 1970s the combined forces of government and public outcry created a plethora of environmental legislation that embodied both new and older types of concerns. The Clean Air Act, the establishment of the Environmental Protection Agency, and other similar legislation and policy decisions reflected the renewed interest of an American public concerned with pollution, the quality of life in urban areas, and the long-term health of the nation's physical environment. The National Wild and Scenic Rivers Act of 1968, an indirect result of the Wilderness Act of

1964, led the way. Legislation such as the Wild Horse and Burro Act of 1971 and the Endangered Species Act of 1973, both of which protected animals from human action and were controversial almost from the moment of passage, illustrated both the optimism of the immediate post-World War II era and the utopianism of the 1960s. These two currents— embodying an increasing unification of pollution issues with historical concerns about wilderness, wild land, and animal issues—were at times contradictory and at other times indistinguishable. They created a consensus about the environment that lasted throughout the 1970s and ended only with the inauguration of Ronald Reagan in 1981.

QUALITY OF LIFE ISSUES AND REGULATION

The twentieth century has been called the regulatory century, and issues of environmental management became a leading example of the trend toward greater government involvement that dominated the first eighty years of the century. Since the Progressive era at the turn of the century, the federal government played an ever-growing role in regulating a range of industries; everything from food to manufacturing became subject to regulation, and companies and industries that did not abide by the new rules often experienced swift and heavy sanction. Most of the federal bureaucracies that managed land were established during this era, and some developed a range of power over the activities of the groups that utilized resources. The New Deal of the 1930s helped make the government the source of solutions to all kinds of social problems because it was the only solvent entity in the nation for much of the decade. By the end of World War II, the role of government in social and economic affairs, in particular its regulatory functions, had been well established in the United States. Although some quarters of society retained a sometimes fierce resistance, Americans generally expected federal support for a range of programs to come with stipulations attached.

But nothing prepared Americans for the expansion of the federal role in the postwar era. By the 1960s new environmental regulations were near the top of the list of changes that had occurred in everyday American life. New categories of rules and laws, aimed at making the shared areas of American life—the roads, parks, factories, and neighborhoods of the nation—more habitable were added to the lists of regulations for federal land. Although there was notable interest in creating new regulations throughout the 1950s, much of the impetus for this transformation followed 1960. Traditional environmental issues such as wilderness were the first to be sanctioned in the legal code, quickly followed by the regulation of pollution of the kind that fouled the beaches of Santa Barbara, California, by placing limits on the way in which commodities such as oil were transported. Soon pollution, a metaphor for the quality of daily life, became the focus of some aspects of the environmental movement because legislators could assuage the public with antipollution legislation.

Quality of life issues—as this complex and amorphous matrix of ideas, attitudes, and responses came to be known—reflected the changing nature of postwar American life. During the 1960s the United States was a particularly optimistic society, willing to undertake challenges such as disease and poverty in its midst. Young Americans especially developed strong utopian tendencies, seeing the promise of America as unfulfilled and the world as perfectible by their efforts. A cleaner environment—a response to the gross fouling of the continent that was linked to the great burst of economic prosperity that followed World War II—seemed a reasonable goal for a powerful, affluent society. Americans had the wealth and the desire to think as much about the future condition of their nation as about its present condition, a situation that spawned much of the optimism that was evident at every level of U.S. society.

ECONOMIC PROBLEMS AND ENVIRONMENTALISM

As Americans prepared to tackle the consequences of their prosperity, they ran up against hard economic realities that threatened the prosperity of the nation. As a result of the combined effects of

Vietnam War-era inflation and the Organization of Petroleum Exporting Countries (OPEC) embargo of the United States in the aftermath of the Arab-Israeli Yom Kippur War of 1973, both the optimism and the liberal social policies of the 1960s came under severe attack. The physical manifestations of such change were widespread, but the impact on the American psyche was even greater.

After the end of the OPEC embargo, gasoline and heating oil prices increased as much as 33 percent, and availability became limited. Long lines at gasoline stations chilled the blood of anyone raised with the ethic that an automobile meant freedom. The rising cost of heating oil threatened the economic stability of middle- and lower-income families, especially in the Northeast, where oil remained the dominant fuel for home heating. Energy conservation became so widely espoused that during the administration of President Jimmy Carter, the thermostats in federal buildings were turned down to sixty-eight degrees Fahrenheit to conserve energy during the winter. The cultural ramifications were even broader, in one instance changing the definition of "room temperature" in cookbooks from seventy-two degrees to sixty-eight degrees Fahrenheit. The impact on recipes remains unclear.

Efforts to conserve energy were closely linked to efforts to defeat inflation, characterized by President Gerald Ford and the WIN ("Whip Inflation Now") button that he frequently wore. Both concepts—the need to fight inflation and the need to conserve energy—suggested real limits that Americans had previously been aware of but had mightily resisted.

These factors helped dampen enthusiasm for programs that were directed at increasing the quality of life. The growth of the American economy slowed dramatically, and in fits and spasms it contracted. The surpluses of the 1960s began to disappear. Not only did the rate of increase in spending for social and environmental programs begin to slow, but also some influential elements in society began to complain about the economic cost of locking up resources. As the results of the 1976 election showed, quality of life to American voters meant economic issues. Nearly 70 percent of voters polled defined the economy as their primary concern, and in an industrial society, economic prosperity came hand in hand with environmental consequences. As the economic climate worsened, few in the industrial hierarchy responded to the challenges. Foreign automobiles, more energy efficient and often cheaper than comparable domestic models, dramatically increased their share of the market while the engineers in Detroit continued to build the same gas-guzzlers that had dominated the landscape since 1945. The lack of response by the auto industry was characteristic; most Americans felt that they faced a situational problem rather than an ongoing problem that would change the way they thought and acted. This was as apparent in the environmental movement as it was in industry. People facing pollution and other environmental problems and their congressional representatives continued to advocate and pass legislation that promoted environmental quality of life issues that were expensive to implement and that had the potential to have an impact on the bottom line of a variety of businesses.

In part, such legislation continued to succeed because few recognized the fundamental nature of the changes in the American economy, preferring to regard the downturn of the mid- and late 1970s as an aberration rather than as a portent of an ominous economic future. Crafting pollution legislation also succeeded because quality of life issues were closely linked to the urban environment, where the overwhelming majority of Americans lived. It was in the cities where the taste of lead from automobile exhaust hung in the air, where factories spewed smoke that darkened the skies and turned white shirts a sooty color, and where water bubbled with suds as dead fish floated atop the foam of detergent- and effluent-filled streams. The Great Lakes were fouled, sewage was routinely dumped into the country's water courses from open pipes, and a thick haze of smog settled, seemingly permanently, over numerous U.S. cities. Americans looked at the cost of their postwar prosperity and collectively determined that something had to be done to improve their living conditions as much as their standard of living. Prosperity had its consequences. Using some of the wealth of a nation that most continued to regard as the most prosperous on earth to mitigate such undesirable by-products as pollution seemed a reasonable solution to an increasingly vexing dilemma that threatened the image of affluence so crucial to the post-1950 nation.

Rachel Carson's public exposure of DDT had been one major catalyst for the new interest in urban environmental issues, but the focus of the battle against pesticides was narrow in comparison with the eventual breadth of interest in environmental quality. Issues such as urban pollution, air quality, water pollution, solid-waste disposal, and the use of urban land attained new significance, regulated in part by the federal government and in part by the rise of the use of zoning as a technique to restrict local uses of land. Using the mechanisms of grass-roots level democracy, citizen groups began to seek to make a difference in the condition of their environment. Mostly middle class, these people were forerunners of a revolution in American thinking and, ultimately, in American policy and law.

By 1965 pollution control had become a major priority of a large segment of the American population, and that priority was soon reflected in the actions of legislators. Ecology as a social concept rather than as a science had become important in American society, and the visible conditions that fouled U.S. cities made certain that people's interest would not flag. Mirroring the spirit of the times, efforts to devise technologies that would create less environmental damage were initiated, but the most significant changes came in law. Beginning with the first pieces of modern pollution regulation legislation, which typically sought to do more than simply spread the damage over a wider area or compensate its victims, the effort slowly gathered momentum.

Water pollution was the first area to be regulated. The Water Pollution Control Act of 1948 set the tone for the first generation of regulatory legislation. It placed most responsibility for pollution control on local government. Public health agencies administered water-quality control, emphasizing the protection of public water supplies from bacteria. The Clean Water Act of 1960 followed the same pattern. The Clean Waters Act of 1966 was emasculated by the oil industry, which successfully preserved its offshore drilling prerogatives at the expense of enforcement clauses in the law. Despite the best of intentions, the law made it nearly impossible for the federal government to sue an oil company that was responsible for a spill. Laws and mechanisms to limit pollution existed, but they rarely had the kind of mandate and force that allowed for genuine enforcement.

The Clean Air Act of 1963 was a case in point. This legislation gave states a way to begin air pollution abatement and allowed the federal government to offer encouragement of the process. Following the lead of earlier water pollution control measures, the act allowed the federal government to intervene only at the request of states. A lackluster enforcement record followed; only eleven abatement cases were filed between 1965 and 1970, much to the consternation of a public that routinely lived with fouled air. Legislation without powerful impact on behavior had been the norm. In the changing cultural climate, it increasingly seemed an insufficient remedy.

THE IMPACT OF NEPA

By the end of the 1960s an urgency began to permeate the nation, particularly concerning pollution. Existing laws were ineffective, and as the nation seemed to change political directions and absorb new cultural values during the last half of the decade, government was seen both as a source of woe and as an agent of change. Those who favored government intervention won out in public policy arenas because in the aftermath of events such as the Santa Barbara oil spill and the noxious air mass over Birmingham, government seemed the one entity that could successfully grapple with powerful interests such as major industries and natural resource conglomerates.

The federal presence in the new environmentalism emerged almost overnight. From somewhere in the remote realm of interest, it quickly became a primary issue on the American agenda. Senators Gaylord Nelson of Wisconsin and Edmund Muskie of Maine took the lead in Congress, and a spate of legislation quickly followed. A reluctant President Richard M. Nixon signed the land-mark National Environmental Policy Act of 1969 (NEPA) after it sailed through Congress as public concern about the environment turned to outrage and as politicians responded to this new concern. The massive support for the act indicated both its great importance and the consensus concerning its necessity; only the most significant and the most widely popular legislative proposals generated such widespread support.

NEPA reflected the environment's importance to American voters. The concept of the environment had become a buzzword with nearly uniform recognition. Americans believed that the protection of their environment was a "good," a socially advantageous and highly desirable goal. The passage of NEPA reflected the public's feelings. It committed the government to "create and maintain conditions under which man and nature can exist in productive harmony, and fulfill the social, economic, and other requirements of present and future generations of Americans." The set of obligations included in this language reflected the dramatic shift in the meaning of the environment to the American public. Front and center, environmental quality had become a standard of measurement in American life.

Among the many provisions of NEPA was the requirement that an environmental impact statement (EIS) be written to describe the impact of every federal or federally supported undertaking. The EIS became the most important document in the process of legal compliance established by the new act. Impact statements compelled federal administrators to make a careful assessment of the consequences of their proposals. The requirement opened their actions to a level of scrutiny that federal administrators had never before experienced; at the same time, it allowed challenges based on the environmental impact of projects. All EIS documents were public record, allowing all those who wanted to look at the rationale that underlay federal decisions to gain an insight into federal decision-making. Under ideal circumstances, the EIS process offered a comprehensive view of the environmental consequences of federal activities to the president, the cabinet, and executive-level advisors. With its requirement of the environmental impact statement, NEPA initiated a new level of accountability in the development of federal projects.

NEPA also created the Council on Environmental Quality (CEQ), the highest legal advisory body to the president on environmental affairs. The CEQ consisted of three members selected by the president and approved by the Senate. Created with an exclusively advisory capacity, the CEQ had its mission thrust upon it by the president. Its role was largely determined by the chief executive, who could make as little or as much use of it as he chose. Initially Nixon did not utilize the CEQ, but members of the council took the initiative and shaped not only the president's legislative agenda on the environment in 1971 and 1972, but also other environmental decisions made during the Nixon administration. Under some leaders and in some administrations, the CEQ was assertive. In other cases, it was decidedly less so.

The emphasis on this new environmentalism spread rapidly and widely. Nixon gave the first "Message on the Environment" to Congress in February 1970—another step mandated by NEPA. Within months, Congress refused to appropriate further funding for the supersonic transport (SST), negating almost one billion dollars of prior investment. At about the same time, Nixon halted the $50 million Cross-Florida Barge Canal, the first peacetime project ever stopped as a result of the environmental impact it would cause. This cessation dealt a thundering blow to the powerful U.S. Army Corps of Engineers, which had expected to build the canal and had rarely before been thwarted. The taint on progress that appeared in the immediate post-World War II period became the topic of national debate on public policy. In the climate of the early 1970s, economic growth and its many impacts would generate much serious discussion.

THE FOUNDING OF EPA

In December 1970 the signature event of the environmental revolution—the founding of the Environmental Protection Agency (EPA)—took place. Established under the auspices of NEPA, EPA

President Richard Nixon signs into law far-reaching anti-pollution legislation. Of this legislation, the establishment of the Environmental Protection Agency (EPA) in December of 1970 ranked as the signal moment of the environmental movement. Applauding the President's actions is Russell E. Train, chairman of the Council on Environmental Quality.

was created as the centerpiece of the emerging federal environmental regulatory system. With the concurrence of Congress, Nixon established the new agency in an effort to centralize the diverse parts of the federal bureaucracy that had responsibility for the administration of environmental affairs. The EPA supplanted agencies such as the Federal Water Quality Administration in the Department of the Interior, which previously had handled water pollution enforcement, and the National Air Pollution Control Administration, located in the Department of Health, Education, and Welfare. EPA also administered the many solid-waste management programs scattered throughout the government, set standards and guidelines for radiation control (a task formerly the province of the Federal Radiation Council), and handled pesticide and toxic substance registration and administration. Created as a "line agency"—one with a budget line all its own (a $2.5 billion budget by 1972) and more than seven thousand employees—EPA was designed to wield a powerful club on behalf of the bipartisan coalition that drove American environmental politics.

With the establishment of EPA, the federal government codified the era's new environmental ethic into both policy and the legal code. Prior to the early 1970s, economic justification was sufficient for any private or public undertaking. Urban renewal, which demolished much of the historic fabric of American cities, proceeded without statutory regulation until 1966, when the Historic Preservation Act was passed. Despite the Clean Air and Clean Water Acts of the 1960s, pollution continued nearly unabated, and air quality continued to worsen. Dams and other public works projects were built with the flimsiest of rationale and with little concern for either their economic or environmental consequences. The creation of EPA sent a different message to the public, one suggesting that new methods of operation would redefine the patterns of administration that governed the use of the American environment. This powerful new agency, with its many ways to compel compliance, signaled the advent of a world in which the federal government and private industry would assess the consequences of their actions before initiating them and would consider alternatives to any damage that might be caused. It was a new era for Americans. The federal government assumed a greater level of responsibility for environmental conditions than previously had been expected or required by law.

But from the environmentalist perspective, the environmental impact statement process contained a number of significant flaws. As one former Department of the Interior specialist later described, the process did not require that destructive actions be stopped. It required only that they be explained. "You could write an environmental impact statement that said the consequence of this action would be to destroy the world and that there were better alternatives than this action and the action could still go forward," remembered the specialist. Environmental impact statements, as were many similar pieces of legislation, were created to serve a certain purpose and were not designed to cover every eventuality. The process did set new levels of requirement that ironically built limits into the very structure of the regulatory process. Environmental impact statements became the most important document in the initiation of a federal undertaking, but sometimes superficial research and faulty reasoning took the place of clear-headed analysis and substantive and comprehensive documentation. The EIS often became a malleable document, shaped to the needs of constituencies that sought development and less useful in resolving environmental issues than the authors of NEPA might have supposed.

But the demand for environmental protection spread widely and gained much political strength. A range of institutions played broad roles in this transformation of values, with the U.S. legal system in the forefront. Sympathetic courts were instrumental in the translation of new environmental sentiment into policy and law. In 1970, in response to a lawsuit over the Alaska Pipeline, federal judges halted the multibillion-dollar, eight hundred-mile-long project as federal officials, environmentalists, and the oil industry attempted to determine what the environmental impact of the pipeline might be. Even after the project was revived in 1972 by the Department of the Interior, it faced ongoing resistance inside and outside of government. Environmentalists challenged any government action concerning the pipeline, while astute individuals within the Department of the Interior advised their superiors not to sign off on the flawed environmental impact statement that had come through the bureaucracy. In the opinion of numerous officials, the EIS did not conform to the strictures of the new regulations, and a signature affirming the statement had the potential to generate a massive lawsuit. A combination of politics, perspective, the courts, and attentive groups and individuals joined forces to make compliance with new laws and regulations a reality.

Negotiating the minefield that environmental protection had become had clear consequences for federal agencies. They faced agitated and involved publics who were more powerful, more diverse, louder, more vociferous than ever before, and more determined to make the federal bureaucracy responsive to their multifaceted demands. The new rules and regulations about conduct and the heightened expectations of the public, administration officials, and the media concerning the condition of the environment made management decisions difficult. Projects that would have barely been noticed a decade before became front-page news. In the new climate, federal officials had to carefully toe the various lines drawn by everyone from industry to the increasingly powerful environmental lobby.

EARTH DAY

The first Earth Day, observed on April 22, 1970, exemplified public response to the idea of an environmentalism based on quality of life. Reflecting both the independent spirit of 1960s politics and the social healing essential to the process of coopting ideas from the American cultural revolution, Earth Day started inauspiciously as a series of environmental teach-ins, formally informal sessions in which people expressed their views at colleges, high schools, and community centers across the country. From these meager beginnings Earth Day metamorphosed into a major American cultural event.

Gaylord Nelson, the U.S. senator from Wisconsin and an outspoken advocate of environmental quality, developed the idea of a "National Teach-in on the Crisis of the Environment" at a

April 22, 1970: The first Earth Day is in full swing at Union Square Park in Manhattan.

September 1969 symposium in Seattle, Washington. Nelson's objectives were twofold: to help crystallize the environmental constituency and to limit its links with the New Left that was so prominent on American college campuses at the time. Nelson believed that the environmental crisis, as the subject of environmental quality was then called, was the greatest dilemma facing the human race, one that transcended social, cultural, political, economic, and geographic boundaries. The teach-in he envisioned would begin the process of alerting everyone to the subject's significance.

By the end of 1969 the idea of the teach-in had generated a great deal of attention. Nelson's office remained at the center of the issue, and a new organization, initially named Environmental Teach-in Inc., was founded to handle queries about the idea. Environmental activists from across the political spectrum became involved as the idea of the teach-in gained currency. "Once I announced the teach-in, it began to be carried by its own momentum," Nelson remembered. "If we had actually been responsible for making the event happen, it might have taken several years and millions of dollars to pull it off. In the end, Earth Day became its own event."

In the hands of its chief organizer, Harvard University law student Denis Hayes, Earth Day became a centrist event. Hayes eschewed the confrontational politics of the New Left, seeking instead to unite the supporters of environmental issues rather than to polarize them. "We didn't want to alienate the middle class," Hayes remarked later. "We didn't want to lose the 'Silent Majority' just because of style issues." Hayes and the other organizers hoped that the decentralized nature of the event would allow it to avoid the confrontational stance that so much of American public life had during the late 1960s. The organizers fashioned a celebration as much as a critique of American society, a search for consensus as well as for alternatives. Although this gave Earth Day the widest possible reach, it cut into support among some of the most activist constituencies. These groups equated militance with activism and found the tempered rhetoric of Earth Day a little tame.

Earth Day was a rousing success. As many as twenty million people around the nation participated. The advocacy group that grew out of the teach-in, Environmental Action, described Earth Day as the largest, cleanest, most peaceful demonstration in American history. Hayes reflected the sentiments of many of the people involved: "We will not appeal any more to the conscience of institutions because institutions have no conscience. If we want them to do what is right, we must make them do what is right. We will use proxy fights, lawsuits, demonstrations, research, boycotts, ballots—whatever it takes. This may be our last chance." Mixing 1960s ideology and the rhetoric of moral suasion with the tactics of the civil rights movement, Hayes fashioned a strategy that simultaneously included and excluded radicalism. In the environmental movement, he seemed to say, all people have a stake, no matter what their politics.

Junior-high students march in the business district of their hometown in a demonstration organized in connection with the first Earth Day, 1970.

The focus of Earth Day became a consensus-oriented form of education. The typical program included a convocation, singing, dancing, food, and rhetoric from environmental advocates. There was also a political dimension; petitions advocating the cessation of local industrial activities that polluted were sometimes circulated, and political candidates who espoused proenvironment values used the event as a podium. The educational effort was also directed at a younger audience in the elementary school grades. In one instance repeated across the country, a sixth-grade class marched outside on a raw April day in Illinois to plant a tree on its playground as a way of participating in the celebration.

This inclusiveness gave the movement wide currency in the nation as the public awoke to the idea of the environment as a social issue. Environmentalism began to compete for the mantle of secular religion in modern American life. Its symbols caught on widely as its message spread throughout the counterculture and the establishment. Americans from all realms embraced the values of environmentalism; politicians and "long hairs" together talked of the same goals. Legislatures followed with supportive action, including the passage of bottle bills, which mandated the return of glass for reuse, and other similar bills. For a brief moment, it seemed as if the broad spectrum of support for environmental quality would heal the immense political rift in American society. Here was an issue that a wide range of Americans, from the leaders of industry to the political left, could embrace as a social objective.

THE LIMITS OF 1970S ENVIRONMENTALISM

But this positive sentiment proved illusory. Although environmentalism generated a great amount of public support and managed to find a home in bipartisan politics in the 1970s, it failed to reach into every corner of American society. Centrism meant many potential adherents, but it also watered down the intensity of environmental support. The raw numbers of people interested in the topic were good for environmentalism, but their interest was not always very deep. Nor did mainstream environmentalism reflect the breadth of the American spectrum. Conspicuous by their absence were minorities—African Americans, Hispanics, and Native Americans in particular—and people from rural areas. Conservationists and environmentalists historically had come from the classes of people who were economically secure. Environmentalism's message about deferring material gain in order to preserve the future held little appeal for the poor or others previously excluded from economic prosperity. Farmers, increasingly dependent on chemical technologies for greater crop yield in the nearly century-old effort to combat the problems of surplus with more surplus, and ranchers, embroiled in a constant struggle to maximize the efficiency of marginal public and private grazing land, were left out of what was essentially an urban-based vision. Environmentalism of the 1970s dealt with issues such as pollution that affected everyone, but often its language and form of presentation spoke to the feelings of city people about distance from the natural world. Despite the emphasis on regulation embodied in legislation such as NEPA and in the founding of EPA, environmentalism retained a number of the traits of mid-century conservation. Its ideology tended to focus on the kind of outdoor issues that had been the province of the Sierra Club and the Wilderness Society even as pollution and urban issues became the focus of public interest and the legislation that inevitably followed.

One result of the historic influence on wilderness and the outdoors was the Endangered Species Act of 1973. Species extinction had been one of the consequences of the attitudes of Americans toward wildlife. A recurring theme in American literature since James Fenimore Cooper wrote during the 1820s and 1830s, the wanton destruction of wildlife accompanied the Euro-American march across the continent. A range of species, including the most famous, the passenger pigeon that once crowded American skies, was eliminated, and numerous other species teetered on the brink of oblivion. Even the ubiquitous prairie dog, once seemingly everywhere, was reduced to a relict population.

Legislation to protect the most threatened species was first passed during the middle of the 1960s. The Endangered Species Preservation Act of 1966 was another of the prototypes for environmental legislation. It provided for the protection and propagation of native species of fish and wildlife, from the largest vertebrates to even the minuscule Devil's Hole pupfish, a fish less than two inches long that lived in one sinkhole in Ash Meadows, Nevada. A subsequent bill, the Endangered Species Conservation Act of 1969, expanded protection from vertebrates to mollusks and crustaceans as it extended the range of species covered from only those endangered to those threatened by humanity. The

Endangered Species Act of 1973 became the final stage in the process of developing protective legislation. This act reaffirmed the importance of habitat protection, although not without controversy. It focused on the protection of "critical habitat," but did not define "critical" in any sort of legal or administrative context. A battle over semantics resulted in which economic and environmental needs were uncomfortably juxtaposed.

The Endangered Species Act made national headlines during construction of the Tellico Dam on the Little Tennessee River in the mid-1970s. When University of Tennessee zoology professor David Etnier discovered a small fish called the snail darter in the Little Tennessee River in the area that would be flooded behind the nearly completed $116 million dam project, a test of the ethic of bipartisan environmentalism began. A two-year legal battle over continuation of dam construction ensued. Although the Endangered Species Act was widely blamed for the cessation of work on the dam, an interagency committee found that the dam was also a classic piece of pork barreling, a project with no economic feasibility other than to provide jobs in the district of a powerful congressional representative.

In the end, President Carter, already locked in a battle over water resource development projects, signed "with regret" the public works appropriations bill to which a provision that effectively exempted the Tellico Dam from all laws had been added as much of Congress snoozed. So unsure were proponents of the dam that this political maneuver would stand a legal challenge that twelve hours after Carter's signature the bulldozers were at work, completing the destruction of the habitat of this unique creature. For the moralistic and sensitive Carter, this was a brutal decision because it pitted his beliefs against pragmatic politics. Politics, as usual, won. Even in friendly hands, the Endangered Species Act proved weaker than supporters had hoped.

The Tellico Dam situation highlighted some of the difficulties that Carter faced as he tried to implement an environmentally sophisticated political agenda. He saw the world in moralistic terms, taking clearly articulated but sometimes politically unsophisticated stances on a range of environmental issues. In cases

such as Tellico Dam and in his efforts to cut funding for a number of water resource development projects, the president ran up
against entrenched congresspeople and powerful federal agencies. One critic of the federal water system, author Marc Reisner,
has suggested that the Tennessee Valley Authority (TVA), which
had "evolved from a benevolent paternalism into the biggest
power producer, biggest strip miner, and single biggest polluter in
the United States," had become "unaccountable to the public
[and] largely unaccountable to Congress." In this climate, a well-
intentioned president could be and was easily trapped by those
more experienced in the wily tactics necessary to bring home
even the wasteful projects that helped prop up local economies.
Caught between doing what he thought was right and keeping
the government moving, Carter made more enemies than friends
with his forays into environmental policy.

The Tellico Dam controversy also affected the reauthorization
of the Endangered Species Act in 1978. Legislative renewal
occurred during the middle of the controversy, and as a result of
the fray congressional reauthorization added a number of factors
to the assessment process. Most of these factors were economic
in nature, related to the conditions surrounding projects rather
than to the biological factors built into the initial bill. The application of the Endangered Species Act in a changing economic
climate resulted in a weakening of its power.

AN ENERGIZED PUBLIC

In the early 1970s issues such as wilderness continued to inspire
the greatest response from the American public. Wilderness had
an iconographic meaning that gave it millions of armchair supporters, and changing technology gave many more people the
opportunity to seek wilderness experiences. The combination
of several factors—easier mobility along interstate highways, better equipment and technology for outdoor activities, and a heightened sense that quality of life included issues such as pitting
oneself against nature and learning to appreciate the natural

world—created a revolution in American recreation. With access to lightweight gear, more comfortable clothing and footwear, and better-tasting freeze-dried food, Americans made wilderness in particular and the outdoors in general fashionable.

Americans translated their growing interest in the outdoors into involvement in environmental organizations. Many environmental groups doubled or tripled in size in a brief period. A vociferous segment of the public—energized by the enactment of legislation, confident in a value system that challenged authority, and suspicious of the pronouncements of government in the aftermath of the Johnson administration's loss of credibility over Vietnam and the fall of Nixon in the Watergate scandal—began to play a much more significant role in questions concerning wilderness as well as in environmental affairs in general.

The range of legislation passed in the first years of the environmental decade facilitated public involvement in environmental issues. The spate of new bills covered nearly every possible aspect of environmental management, from the Wild Horse and Burro Act of 1971 to the Fishery Conservation and Management Act of 1976. The environmental impact statement process required publication of draft documents and public comment on the proposed legislation. Development soon faced challenges not only from local people directly affected by changes in environmental policy, but also from a national constituency that might complain about federal decisions. Despite the fact that it was sometimes flawed, the comment process allowed and even encouraged a level of public participation that had not previously existed. It energized the public, made it feel a part of decision-making, and gave environmental issues a public constituency and a widened audience.

This new situation created severe management problems for federal agencies. Weakened by their bouts with an energized public and seeking to please the loudest voices around them, federal agencies ran up against the management problems inherent in the issue of wilderness. In case after case, federal administrative decisions that evaluated areas covered by the description of potential wilderness in the Wilderness Act were challenged by a range of interest groups. In New Mexico, a National Park Service recommendation of "no wilderness" at Bandelier National Monument was defeated by a vociferous public that included people from across the country. Ironically, a significant number of supporters of the wilderness revealed that they did not understand the parameters of legally designated wilderness when they supported it; they advocated the inclusion of developed areas within the boundaries of the designated wilderness—a clear contravention of the Wilderness Act. On the Navajo reservation, challenges to the Peabody Coal Company's EIS for a slurry pipeline to carry coal eventually led to an increase from the pre-EIS price of $5 per acre-foot for water to a more realistic assessment of the impact of the one-way pipeline off the reservation, a cost of $600 per acre-foot implemented in 1987. The Forest Service faced repeated attacks on its wilderness policy as its officials tried to maximize the timber cut from national forests at the same time that segments of the public sought to preserve as much roadless land in designated wilderness areas as possible. In the early 1970s frustrated foresters developed a comprehensive review process, the Roadless Area Review and Evaluation (RARE) in response to the situation.

After 1972 RARE proceeded rapidly. Areas of roadless forested land throughout the country were evaluated for their appropriateness as wilderness areas. The Forest Service adopted a three-alternative system: an inventory produced areas that the agency determined were suitable for wilderness and others that its reviewers thought unsuitable. The areas that remained were slated for further study. The agency was caught between powerful special interests. The timber industry became incensed when what its members regarded as valuable timber was locked up in USFS proposals to designate wilderness, while wilderness proponents believed that too many roads were planned and that too much timber was to be cut. The tension became particularly fierce over areas for which further study was planned. Wilderness proponents especially saw this intermediate category as a prelude to cutting, fearing the political power of the timber industry and its strong ties to Congress. Timber companies did not understand the sentiments that opposed their position and regarded their opponents as merely and unjustly antibusiness. Weakened by the ramifications of the political and cultural climate of the 1960s, which increased the vulnerability of federal agencies, the Forest Service vacillated. RARE became unpopular across the board. No one was happy with the results of the process.

Forest Service officials determined to try again. Assistant Secretary of Agriculture Rupert M. Cutler and U.S. Forester John R. McGuire initiated a second roadless area review program, called RARE II, that sought to include the widest possible public participation. Again good intentions blew up in the agency's face; the public meetings that foresters so wanted became tumultuous and contentious as the changing economic climate—burdened by post-Vietnam War inflation and the increase in fuel prices caused by the OPEC oil embargo—cut the margin that separated success and failure for timber companies and ranchers to a minimum.

The cries of the new environmental coalition a few years before had not seemed threatening. But by the mid-1970s everyone in a range of industries felt that entire ways of living and earning a livelihood were on the line. Too much resentment and not enough constructive input about the selection process followed. The range of special interests that demanded their slice of the Forest Service pie seemed even larger and more unmanageable than ever before. Finding a middle ground among the various constituencies became even more difficult as the Forest Service, weakened by the changing political climate and new rules governing the behavior of federal agencies, sought to serve disparate and usually mutually exclusive interests.

Part of the problem that the Forest Service faced was its longstanding emphasis on commercial economic uses of national forest land at a time when a large segment of the American public espoused a more holistic approach to the use of natural resources. Tied to the ethos of Progressivism, the Forest Service, at its core, still believed in regulated management of natural resources, the principle articulated by Gifford Pinchot more than seventy years before. Pinchot had brilliantly shaped public opinion; his successors reacted to the demands of the environmental public and the timber industry, both of which sought to mold agency policy to their objectives. Meeting the demands of this new political and cultural setting, the heightened environmental awareness, and the more strident demands of industry meant throwing over the basic tenets of the agency. It was a step that foresters were not prepared to take.

The result squeezed the Forest Service between the powerful and vocal environmental public on one side and timber companies on the other. After 1960, when it enacted the doctrine of multiple use, the Forest Service had straddled the line between the increasingly active public and the industries that had been instrumental parts of its base of support. The increase in recreational use of national forests and the growing primacy of outdoor experience in American culture forced the agency to make choices that it had always hoped to avoid.

When the Forest Service selected only fifteen million acres of the recommended thirty-six million acres to be preserved as wilderness under RARE II, all sides exploded in fury. Traditional wilderness and timber industry adversaries all protested at what they described as the destruction of their interests. The recreation industry split; some factions advocated wilderness as the most efficacious and profitable approach, whereas others advocated development as the basis for growth of the industry. Hunters and off-road vehicle enthusiasts attacked designated wilderness as a threat to their interests. In the gale-force winds that resulted, the Forest Service tried to hold on to its position.

ENVIRONMENTALISM AND NEW ECONOMIC REALITIES

The multifaceted debate over the RARE II program, the reauthorization of the Endangered Species Act, and a host of other environmental situations reflected the changing tone of U.S. life during the late 1970s. As long as the American economy continued to expand, or at least as long as the perception that opportunity was growing was commonly accepted, the removal of resources from potential production was a possibility. Conditioned by the economic successes of the 1950s and 1960s, Congress became accustomed to, in effect, apportioning the pie that was the American economy. Most resources were directed toward production, but a few resources, particularly spectacular scenery and remote places, could be designated for spiritual, recreational, and other not inherently or evidently profitable uses. It was the mark of a "civilized" and mature society that understood its technological limits, many thought, evidence of a compassionate and rational culture that could also advocate ideas such as the end of poverty in America for all time.

But after the OPEC oil embargo and in the middle of inflation inspired by the Vietnam War, the nation's belief in ever-expanding prosperity began to wane. Coupled with the increase in expectations across the nation that accompanied the great economic aberration between 1945 and 1973, the end of the widely held perception of eternal plenty posed a problem for advocates of environmentalism. Its values spoke to a different range of sentiments than did historic patterns of economic endeavor. These were differences that could be tolerated during periods of prosperity but that were easily challenged as the economy stagnated. The goals of environmentalism seemed to be class-based and insensitive to more basic concerns, particularly among traditional, heavy-industry, blue-collar employees, whose jobs became scarce and whose replacement employment came at tremendous decrease in remuneration.

At the same time, a new and far more ominous threat to the quality of life appeared in American society. As traditional industries slowed their growth, reorganized to the detriment of their blue-collar workforces, and prepared themselves for foreign competition, the toxic consequences of their operations came increasingly to the attention of the American public. Both hazardous waste and nuclear waste were recognized as threats not only to the American way of life, but also to people's faith in their institutions. Such waste seemed omnipresent; industry, the military, and even Silicon Valley, the high-tech hope for the future of the American economy, produced a seemingly endless list of radioactive and nonradioactive hazardous by-products.

When confronted with evidence of this reality, the public's belief in the system, already damaged by political scandal, took another beating. As the 1980s began, the growing distrust of politics in the post-Watergate era extended even deeper into American society.

Chapter 6

Risk and Culture: Nuclear Power, Hazardous Waste, the Superfund, and the Concept of "Environmental Justice"

By the 1980s subsurface fears regarding the environmental consequences of progress crystallized throughout American society. Americans recognized ever-present threats to their hard-won patterns of life that were broader and even more dangerous than the pollution in the air and in the water around them. The oil spill at Santa Barbara, the smog and haze that by the late 1970s affected even the vistas at the Grand Canyon, and the pollution so evident across the American landscape were easily identified and quantified, measured, and they inspired appropriate reactions. But there were other, more insidious threats that could not be seen with the eye, such as air pollution or litter, and were only apparent after the fact. Growing mistrust of government and a series of incidents brought toxic waste and nuclear power to the center of American debates over the issue of quality of life. Revelations such as the discovery of subsurface toxic sludge beneath a neighborhood and its school in Love Canal, New York, in the mid-1970s and the accident at the Three-Mile Island nuclear reactor in Pennsylvania in 1979 raised serious questions about the social cost of progress and the responsibilities of government, business, and industry. These dilemmas forced Americans to confront fears that they had kept to themselves throughout the post-World War II era and compelled the nation to address difficult and often unanswerable questions about the direction of U.S. society and the patterns of life that Americans valued as a people and as individuals. These fears were transformed as American culture changed, as people responded to the atomic bomb and faced a seemingly endless list of environmental threats that were the result of business practices, government programs, and the sheer greed of individuals, companies, federal agencies, and other actors on the American stage. The threats seemed to multiply; first there were aboveground atomic and nuclear bomb blasts, then Rachel Carson exposed the hidden effects of pesticides. Soon after, poorly sited and designed nuclear reactors, contaminated soil and groundwater, PCBs, and other insidious chemicals and compounds attracted public attention. Entire industries were indicted by public perception, including the chemical industry, the petroleum refining industry, and the atomic and nuclear power industries. With its enormous stockpiles of toxic and nuclear material, its sometimes shoddy management, and its overarching penchant for secrecy, the U.S. military also became an evident culprit.

The evidence of the danger was easily visible. Pockets of contamination throughout the nation seemed uninhabitable. Parts of the most heavily industrialized areas of the Louisiana and east Texas coasts were labeled "Cancer Alley" by the media after the rates of cancer among residents soared as full-scale development of chemical and refining facilities occurred. Sections of the Nevada desert where above-ground nuclear weapons testing had taken place were permanently closed to the public. When a mysterious disease killed a number of delegates at an American Legion meeting in Philadelphia in July 1976 and when a few years later highly toxic PCBs, present as a cooling agent in almost every electrical transformer, were created by the combustion of other materials in a building fire in Buffalo, New York, it seemed that the very essence of the modern world had become potentially lethal. The technology that made possible the abundance that Americans enjoyed also had consequences that people feared. Hazardous and nuclear waste came to represent the downside of industrial prosperity.

ATOMIC AND NUCLEAR TESTING

This fear dated from the explosion of the atomic bomb in 1945 and continued, often unspoken but continuous, as it permeated the postwar era's economic growth, politics, and, ultimately, culture. From the beginning of the atomic age—the moment when Italian expatriate scientist Enrico Fermi manipulated control rods in the first exponential pile of uranium and graphite under the stands of Amos Alonzo Stagg Stadium on the University of Chicago campus in December 1942—scientists understood that they were working with a procedure that contained greater power than they had ever before encountered. They recognized that they had begun to harness the forces that make up the universe, but at the time no one really knew where it would lead.

During World War II these scientists sought to utilize that power for military purposes. Science became a wartime tool, and, supported by the investment of vast amounts of federal money, the research drive that began under those stadium stands continued to the Trinity Site in southern New Mexico, where the first atomic device was tested on July 16, 1945, and finally to Hiroshima and Nagasaki, where the power of atomic fission was demonstrated to the world. Even some scientists were astonished at how well their experiment worked; others were surprised that the world survived, believing that there was a strong possibility that an atomic explosion would ignite the entire atmosphere of the earth. Their response, like that of the public, was a combination of exhilaration that the war against Japan had ended and horror at how victory finally had been achieved.

This ambivalence was articulated in many ways in American society. Americans had difficulty understanding the scope of the atomic bomb. To a nation whose people had no way to fathom the remarkable impact of this new technology and had little personal experience with the devastation of war, the bomb was difficult to fathom. The use of the A-bomb was either the end of civilization or a precursor to a world without war. Some abhorred its use. Albert Einstein remarked: "I wish I were a locksmith" instead of a scientist. The eminent American diplomat and politician John Foster Dulles remarked that the atomic bomb and what he called "Christian statesmanship" were hardly compatible; even the repulsive Nazi leader Hermann Göring, architect of the V-1 rockets than rained so much death on the people of Great Britain, reacted to the use of the atomic bomb. "A mighty accomplishment," this mass murderer told reporters from his cell in Nuremberg, West Germany. "I don't want anything to do with it." The atomic bomb had been developed in Los Alamos, New Mexico, far from the scrutiny of the public. After the war, the name "Los Alamos" became tainted by association with the location where atomic technology was developed. When the Los Alamos Ranch School-a popular boarding school for difficult children of the wealthy that had preceded the Manhattan Project on the mesas of northern New Mexico-contacted its extensive waiting list of prospective students about enrolling in a similarly named school at a location near Taos, New Mexico, there was no interest. The very words "Los Alamos" had been stigmatized.

Yet atomic energy was considered essential in the postwar era, first for weaponry in the ensuing Cold War and later for civilian power needs. After the explosion of the first Soviet atomic device on August 29, 1949, an arms race began in earnest. The United States had a significant lead; Americans began testing atomic devices in the South Pacific's Bikini Islands in 1946. Operation Crossroads, the name for these initial tests, utilized fruit flies, goats, pigs, and rats in an effort to determine the impact of radiation on humans. An underwater test called Test Baker in the Crossroads sequence brought especially surprising results. Scientists had assumed that the high levels of fallout would exist for only a few days following a bomb blast. Everything in the blast area, from the ships known as "target vessels" to the tuna in the water, showed continued high levels of radiation. Even the scrubbing that was thought at the time to remove radioactivity did not diminish the levels. To the surprise of scientists, the soldiers sent in with buckets and brushes to scrub away the effects did not at all reduce the levels of radiation on the tested vessels. Task force physician David Bradley concluded in his 1948 book, *No Place to Hide,* that for fallout from nuclear explosions there were "no satisfactory countermeasure and methods of decontamination." In 1949 the two hundred Marshall Islanders who had been evacuated from Bikini Atoll were told that they would never be allowed to return to their homes. Radiation was a powerful by-product of atomic technology with a legacy that proved to be uncontrollable.

Above-ground testing, both in the Bikini Islands and in the Nevada desert, became the rule during the massive Cold War arms buildup of the 1950s and early 1960s. This buildup was both in technological capability and size as bombs became more sophisticated, more numerous, and more powerful. Much of the testing was done to flex national muscle, to demonstrate to the Soviets as they demonstrated to us that each side had the capability to destroy the other with a dazzling array of atomic and later nuclear weapons. The Nevada Test Site—as the location roughly ninety miles from the budding resort and gaming community of Las Vegas became known—was the scene of numerous above-ground tests throughout the 1950s and early 1960s, until above-ground testing was internationally banned in 1963. After that date, tests continued below ground, the occasional rumble of the earth indicating their occurrence to residents of a wide region around the facility. In the Bikinis, above-ground testing continued until the ban came into force. The United States exploded the first thermonuclear device, a Los Alamos-engineered device called Shrimp, there on March 1, 1954, typifying the willingness to experiment with this remote geography. Testing in both places left a radioactive legacy that would persist for at least ten thousand years, later prompting the characterization of such places as "national sacrifice zones."

In the United States, civilian uses of nuclear power lagged behind military uses in large part because the nation had abundant resources for conventional power generation. President Dwight D. Eisenhower developed an "Atoms for Peace" plan; he wanted to use atomic bombs for construction as well as for electricity "too cheap to meter." This decision led to efforts to reshape the remote Alaska coastline with atomic bombs, among other questionable uses of this devastating technology. In the chaos that resulted, nuclear development slowed, and conventional forms

A photographer catches the rising mushroom cloud after the March 12, 1955 detonation of a nuclear device on a 300-foot tower of Yucca Flat at the Nevada Testing Site. Notice the spectators, who feel perfectly safe watching from the grandstands.

of energy generation experienced a revival. As late as the early 1960s, significant construction of coal-fired power plants took place to augment hydroelectric power as a source of American electricity; the massive coal-fired plant on the Navajo reservation at Page, Arizona, which began generation in 1964, was typical. But even with the opening of such plants, nuclear power already was seen as a viable option. In 1957, the year of the Soviet Sputnik launch—perceived as a great challenge to American technological leadership—construction began on the first American nuclear power plant at Shippingsport, Pennsylvania, near Pittsburgh. Three other plants, in Illinois, Massachusetts, and New York, were begun before 1961. The USS *Savannah*, the first nuclear-powered merchant ship, was built at about the same time. By the middle of the 1960s nuclear power sources began to account for much of the new power plant construction and an increasing percentage of power produced in the United States. In 1967, 46 percent of the sixty million kilowatts of electric power orders placed by domestic industry came from nuclear sources.

This increase in nuclear power-generated electricity was one result of a boom in reactor construction. Nuclear power became more attractive as concern with air pollution increased; along with automobiles, coal-fired industry was one of the most virulent polluters. The conversion to nuclear power meant cleaner air, cheaper power as the cost of both coal and gasoline rose, and a seemingly endless source of power as concern about diminishing fossil fuel resources increased. Federal funding supported the construction of nuclear plants, and during the 1960s and 1970s half of all power plants under construction were nuclear. By the late 1970s nearly sixty civilian nuclear power plants were in operation in the United States.

The harnessing of the power of the atom had occurred in rapid fashion, but the consequences of that harnessing had never really been assessed in any public setting. The Atomic Energy Commission, a precursor of the Nuclear Regulatory Commission and the Department of Energy, operated in almost total secrecy. Even above-ground testing within the continental United States received only minimal scrutiny. During the height of the Cold

War, secrecy existed for genuine reasons of national security, but it was no barrier to making heinous decisions; as the threat of imminent nuclear conflict eased after the Cuban Missile Crisis in 1962, the idea of national security was easy to invoke as a way to cloak questionable, irresponsible, and sometimes even unethical behavior.

The consequence was a dangerous degree of risk resulting from atomic and nuclear projects, especially those of the largely unsupervised military. Even in instances when military and federal officials possessed reasonable prior knowledge of the consequences of such atomic testing, there was little effort to address the problems that such testing created. No one assured the safety of those who came in daily contact with radioactive material. Workers at the Hanford Reservation in Washington state, where nuclear weapons were assembled, ran significant risks in the workplace; "downwinders"—people who lived in the path of the winds that blew across the Nevada desert after above-ground testing, across the Hanford Reservation, and even across such seemingly innocuous places as the Oak Ridge National Laboratory outside Knoxville, Tennessee—also ran high health risks. The people who lived in a wide area around the Rocky Flats Arsenal in Colorado—where throughout the postwar era poor monitoring and inadequate storage led to a series of leaks of chemical and atomic material into the surrounding environment—were also in danger. Unexplained and sometimes uncontrolled releases of radiation poisoned cattle and sheep in an area that stretched from the location of testing as far north and east as Minnesota and led to unusually high rates of atypical cancers as well as to clusters of rare diseases among residents of central Washington state, southern Utah, and other places throughout the seemingly bucolic American West.

But in the 1950s and early 1960s workers and private citizens had a hard time getting a hearing for their complaints against the military. Risk in the workplace was not new, but the tone of the Cold War era, highlighted by the rise of Senator Joseph McCarthy and the specious charges of widespread communism that he leveled, mitigated against thorough investigation of the consequences of exposure to radiation. The cultural climate in the United States during the Cold War made it seem unpatriotic to complain, and there were few precedents for challenging government actions or procedures. Like other American employees in heavy industry, people in the proximity of atomic material production—workers, their families, and others—were expected to bear the risk without question or quarrel. Such risk was part of the workplace, one of the social assumptions that governed employer-employee relations, and in an era when Americans felt that their interests were threatened by powerful and malevolent external forces, most were willing to bear their misery in private as part of that sense of patriotic duty.

The silence was compounded by the length of time that passed between most cases of mild radiation exposure and later illness, as well as the subsequent difficulty of proving such relationships with scientific certainty. Although the decision not to return the Bikini Islanders to their home and the pronouncements of federal scientists that the impact of radiation testing on people would take as much as twenty-five years of observation to discern showed that this was a long-term problem, the nature of American decision-making obscured the issues. Americans, then and now, respond to immediate concerns but have trouble planning for the longer term. As long as large numbers of people did not receive immediate lethal exposure, the combination of secrecy and lack of urgency made significant protest and government action or remedies a remote prospect.

ANTINUCLEAR SENTIMENT

The American cultural revolution of the 1960s altered the set of suppositions that had previously governed atomic and nuclear production. The growing distrust of government and the emphasis on individualism combined with subsurface fears about nuclear power to make its use an issue. The expanding interest in environmentalism created a focus for antinuclear sentiment. The amount of secrecy concerning military use of nuclear power created a pervasive uneasiness, but protesters against nuclear power had relatively little evidence to support their fears. Although studies of the survivors of the atomic bombs at Hiroshima and Nagasaki showed that human exposure to radiation was potentially dangerous, it was difficult to persuade Americans that they risked the same fate. Still, enough of a groundswell occurred, and, combined with the strident perspectives of the era, protests against the construction of nuclear power plants soon began.

The opposition to nuclear power plants took many forms and raised a range of issues. Initial opposition centered on the issue of thermal pollution, not on radioactive releases, waste, or the prospects of an accident. The larger reactors that were in vogue by the late 1960s produced a great deal more waste heat than their smaller predecessors. When citizen complaints first came to the Atomic Safety and Licensing Board in 1969, opposition centered on the unwillingness of the board to consider the adverse effect of waste heat on aquatic life. The next battle was bureaucratic; states tried to set a lower standard of tolerance for the release of radionuclides (a radioacive species of atom characterized by the constitution of its nucleus, protons, and energy content), into water than the Atomic Energy Commission (AEC) approved. Even though one of the major builders of reactors, Westinghouse Corporation, announced that it could guarantee zero emissions, the AEC refused to yield to the states what the commission regarded as its prerogative to set standards.

This style of opposition opened the way for more-comprehensive attacks on the idea of civilian nuclear power. The most potent of these focused on the prospect of a nuclear accident of serious proportions. By the early 1970s a significant number of nuclear physicists and engineers offered the perspective that the AEC was too friendly to industry and paid too little attention to public safety. Headed by physicist Henry Kendall of the Kendall Foundation, some of them formed the Union of Concerned Scientists, which provided scientific data for public antinuclear—or "antinuke," as they came to be called—groups. Protests against the construction of nuclear power plants began. The Diablo Canyon reactor, astride the San Andreas fault in California, was the subject of widespread protest, as was the Shoreham plant on Long Island, New York, where there was no adequate evacuation plan for the residents of Long Island in case of an emergency, and the Seabrook plant in New Hampshire.

By the middle of the 1970s there was a schism down the middle of American society concerning nuclear power. On one side were proponents—the industry and other advocates who believed that there are technological solutions to any kind of problem that erupts in front of humanity. Some proponents even believed that technological innovation is the catalyst to creating new opportunities, economic and otherwise, for the human race. On the other side were people who believed that this technology or its application was too dangerous, who saw the risks involved with this cheap—and from a conventional pollution standpoint—clean source of energy as too great for the benefit. This was a conflict of values and belief systems that science could not solve because both points of view depended on mutually exclusive premises. The debate migrated to the realm of politics.

The battle over nuclear power became a battle over the risks that a democratic society might bear to assure its standard of living. The whole cost of coal-fired power sources was great in terms of air pollution, haze, and particulate matter in the air. Nuclear power was supposed to provide an alternative, and as long as the plants that produced electricity worked properly, it succeeded. But changes in the American populace—the newfound distrust of government, the growing fear of technological fixes, and the growing emphasis of environmentalism on quality of life—made for an important double-bind for nuclear power. The majority of Americans wanted their convenience at almost all costs, but collectively they decided that the potential risk of nuclear power outweighed its benefits. They began to show this in demonstrations at facilities such as Shoreham and Diablo Canyon, and the language of opposition soon permeated American society. Although conservative social scientists and economists decried what they termed fallacious reasoning, the nation swung away from nuclear power. In the face of such powerful public opposition, American politicians bowed to the wishes of their constituents. The change became quickly evident. Every order for a nuclear power plant placed in the United States after 1974 was subsequently canceled.

THREE-MILE ISLAND

The worst fears of the public were confirmed on March 28, 1979, when a partial meltdown of the core of Unit 2 of the Metropolitan Edison Co. nuclear reactor on Three-Mile Island in Pennsylvania occurred. The accident began with a simple mechanical function that shut the reactor down. Water pumps cooled the system, but a pressure relief valve opened, allowing water and steam to escape into the reactor's containment system. For two hours, the relief valve remained open as one of the water-level gauges stuck; workers did not notice that anything was amiss. By the end of that period, more than one million gallons of cooling water had been directed away from the core, and the top half of the one hundred-ton uranium fuel core had no water to cool it. Human error then magnified the problems; workers misinterpreted what had occurred, failed to close the open valve, and shut off an emergency cooling system that could have terminated the accident. As a result, temperatures in the core reached five thousand degrees Fahrenheit, and the top half of the core melted. Two hours after the accident began, operators released a torrent of cooling water into the reactor, and the remainder of the core shattered. In an ongoing effort to cool the core, radioactive steam was released into the atmosphere on at least two occasions during the day. Even twelve hours after the shutdown, the reactor remained as hot as 550 degrees Fahrenheit. The radiation leaks continued.

The public response typified the fear that Americans felt toward nuclear power. Even though the radiation was contained within the reactor structure, schools were closed, people were urged to stay indoors, and farmers were told to keep their stock covered and to feed the cattle stored grain instead of letting them graze. When Pennsylvania's governor, Richard Thornburgh, ordered the evacuation of pregnant women and children from the area in response to ongoing releases of high-level radiation, a near panic ensued. A potentially explosive hydrogen bubble in the damaged reactor and false reports of uncontrolled releases of radiation caused more than two hundred thousand people to flee the area. School children ran home to their parents in tears, families debated what to do, and a pall of panic hung over the region.

Three-Mile Island was the nuclear accident that opponents had long feared and that proponents had argued could never happen, and it was on the front pages of every newspaper in the country as well as the lead story on the national television news for twelve consecutive days. Although no significant amount of radiation was released as a result of the partial meltdown, the accident cost the nuclear power industry much more than the one billion dollars in cleanup costs. Three-Mile Island destroyed what remained of American public confidence in nuclear power. It provided a succinct closure to a decade that had been disastrous for public perceptions of American society. The Watergate scandal demolished the remaining trust that the American people had in their government; Three-Mile Island did exactly the same for the nuclear industry.

There had been nuclear power plant accidents before Three-Mile Island, and the far more serious Chernobyl accident in the Soviet Union in 1986 followed, but the Pennsylvania incident served as a turning point for the American power industry. In a strange twist of life imitating art, the Three-Mile Island incident seemed to mirror a 1978 film, *The China Syndrome,* which told the fictional story of the meltdown of a nuclear reactor. Three-Mile Island confirmed the promise of nuclear power as a threat, and no one in the United States could ever fully believe in the industry again. As opponents of nuclear power had feared, an accident had happened. Even though the consequences were minuscule in comparison with what could have occurred, they were sufficient to thoroughly dampen any remaining enthusiasm that the public retained for nuclear power. Tension and hysteria were American responses to nuclear power after Three-Mile Island.

LOVE CANAL

The threat of a nuclear meltdown was only one dimension of the subsurface fears of American society. During the 1970s the prospect of toxic waste buried under homes, schools, and communities also made Americans fearful. Since the beginning of the atomic age, the issue of waste products from nuclear weapons and civilian power production had been largely ignored. The proliferation of the use of chemicals in American society also had unexpected consequences. The image of a silent spring that Rachel Carson had put forward in the early 1960s was only the very tip of potential problems with the toxic by-products of industrial advances. Throughout the nation, industrial wastes were stored, sometimes in adequate facilities, sometimes in rusting fifty-five-gallon barrels. Often chemicals, solvents, and other toxic materials were simply taken to remote rural locations and dumped or buried.

But remote places did not always remain remote. The enormous spread of American cities and the growing value of land around them created a nightmare worthy of science fiction. As suburbs grew and land was platted, people moved into homes unaware that beneath them lay an amalgamation of toxicity that was permeating through the ground, occasionally bubbling up, but always spreading farther—into underground water courses, beneath the places where people lived and worked and where their children played. Occasionally people discovered this threat, but generally they ignored it or did not recognize what they encountered. It was bound to reach up and grab the nation— sooner or later.

The first of what became a seemingly endless list of discoveries occurred in the mid-1970s at Love Canal, near Niagara Falls, New York. During the 1930s and 1940s the Hooker Chemical Company had filled an old hydroelectric canal with industrial waste; a "veritable witches' brew of chemistry, compounds of truly remarkable toxicity" were buried there, according to reporter Michael Brown of the *Niagara Gazette.* In 1953 the company deeded the tract to the Niagara Falls Board of Education for a token payment of one dollar. A school was constructed on the property.

In the following two decades a neighborhood grew up around the old canal. The school was built, but it was moved eighty feet when workers struck a drainage ditch that gave off noxious odors. Work crews later discovered a waste pit. Families began to move into the area surrounding the school. An ordinary neighborhood took shape. It was largely made up of chemical and industrial plant workers and their families, typical of Niagara Falls in their economic situation, educational level, and almost every other form of demography. They were also beholden to the industries that provided their livelihood.

Until the early 1970s there seemed to be nothing terribly unusual about the Love Canal neighborhood. In 1958 three children were burned by exposure to chemical residues on the surface of the canal, but no one detected any pattern of danger. Children played in the debris atop the filled-in canal. Chunks of phosphorus, which the children called "fire rocks," were favored; thrown against cement, they would explode, sending off a trail of white sparks. During hot weather, occasional spontaneous eruptions of fire occurred, coupled with small explosions. There was a persistent odor to the area, but in a heavily industrialized community this was to be expected. Despite these warning signs, no one seemed terribly concerned. Love Canal was only one of many lower-middle-class communities, populated with the families of first-generation homeowners indebted to the paint, chemical, pesticide, and related industries that gave them the opportunity to achieve the American Dream.

More ominous was a pattern of illness and birth defects in the area. When looked at as a group, youngsters in the Love Canal area had more than the usual childhood ailments and more frequent incidences of disease. Deafness was overrepresented among neighborhood children. Birth defects and miscarriages were more common than among the rest of the American population. A disproportionate number of women in the area were treated for a range of cancers. Even the pets reflected the toxicity of the area;

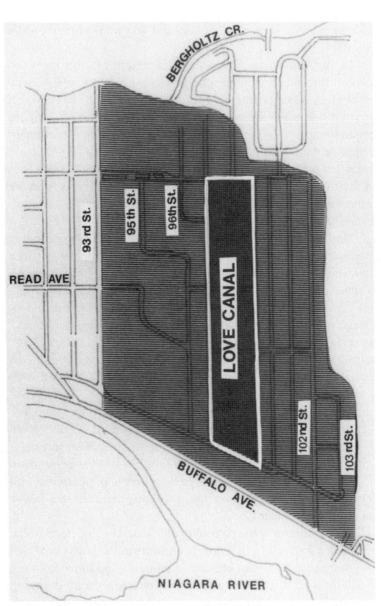

A map of the Love Canal area shows the canal that was filled with industrial waste, and the neighborhood that grew up around it. 1029 families were eventually evacuated from the area that is shown darkened on the map.

lesions on the skin of cats and dogs were common, as were internal tumors. Something was clearly amiss.

As in many similar situations, these maladies at first seemed to result from mere bad fortune. Only after the area received closer scrutiny did a relationship between the buried waste dump and the area's health problems become apparent. The ailments that permeated the neighborhood surrounding the old dump turned what had seemed to be individual tragedy into a damning pattern. When epidemiologists later began to look at the neighborhood to assess the kinds of ailments that people experienced, the numbers of similar maladies common among residents but rare in the population at large suggested that more than unfortunate genetic combinations afflicted the people of Love Canal.

Local government responded in a fashion that can only be termed as deceitful. Into 1978, representatives from the city of Niagara Falls publicly denied that anything was wrong at Love Canal, but as early as 1976 they had informed state Department of Environmental Conservation that dangerous compounds existed in the neighborhood. City officials had even held secret discussions about the problem with representatives of the Hooker Chemical Company. As early as October 1977, EPA officials advocated evacuating the residents and purchasing some or all of the homes in Love Canal. Only in May 1978 was a report from the EPA released showing that the cancer-causing agent benzene was pervasive in household air in the area. Even after the announcement, the county health commissioner and the city manager of Niagara Falls publicly played down the reality of the threat. Hooker Chemical continued to deny that there was a problem. Only after a persistent campaign by reporter Michael Brown and residents of the area such as organizer Lois Gibbs did the information become public. Shortly after, on August 2, 1978, state Health Commissioner Dr. Robert Whalen declared Love Canal a "great and imminent peril to the health of the general public."

Whalen's declaration changed the tenor of the situation. It had been a secret, a fear that residents harbored but were almost afraid to speak about aloud. The public confirmation by an important state official revealed that the years of basements flooded

Angry members of the Love Canal Homeowners Association organized protests in the wake of the declaration that their neighborhood was a peril.

with oozing sludge, minuscule explosions at night, high rates of illness and birth defects, and other unusual instances were the result of external phenomena and assuredly were not individual problems. Whalen exposed the extent of the issue to the public, and people who had thought that their health problems were only their own instantly recognized that their lives had been threatened by one of the companies that sustained them. Raw and unadulterated anger was the initial response; the people of the Love Canal area lashed out at Hooker Chemical and local governments. This emotion was exacerbated by the lack, at every level of government, of a plan for evacuation and by the failure of local, state, and federal government to purchase the properties—a remarkable oversight in the aftermath of the announcement that what people thought of as their safe neighborhood actually was a dangerous and possibly lethal waste hazard.

The situation at Love Canal took on the characteristics of a science-fiction film. No clear rescue plan emerged in the days following Whalen's announcement, and people in the area were close to panic. Now that the threat to their health had been confirmed, they could not simply go on with their lives. The Love Canal neighborhood seemed like a disaster area. In an irony that juxtaposed the security of institutions with the threat of toxicity, the elementary school atop the dump became a crisis center. Long lines of residents jammed the halls as they waited to have their blood tested. Children cried as their mothers tried as hard as they could to suppress their anguish. Men stayed home from their jobs, afraid to leave for fear of what might transpire while they were gone. Families fought over whether to abandon their property or to wait for an order to evacuate. Was the damage to themselves and their children already done, parents asked, or would waiting a few more days make everything worse? The tension was palpable over the entire neighborhood as Love Canal seemed ready to spiral out of control.

The situation improved for residents when New York Governor Hugh Carey visited on August 7. As Niagara Falls awaited Carey, President Jimmy Carter declared the Hooker Chemical dump site a national emergency. Carey followed the presidential

Signs like these appeared on many houses in the Love Canal neighborhood, meant as a protest against the government's failure to purchase the contaminated property.

action with clear promises to the people of Love Canal. The state would purchase all the affected homes at fair market value. "Don't worry about the banks," he announced. "The state will take care of them." The evacuation and cleanup were soon under way, at an eventual cost of more than $30 million.

Within one year the situation in the immediate vicinity of Love Canal had been brought under control. By the spring of 1979, 237 families had been moved, and a considerable number of homes in the neighborhood were eerily dark at night. Soon after the evacuation began, the state erected a green, eight-foot-high chain-link fence around a six-block section. The neighborhood stood, abandoned and ghostlike, a memorial to the dangers of modern life. Of course, the fence did nothing to stop the subterranean spread of the chemicals buried there.

The ordeal was not yet over for area residents. As the state remediation effort began, more and more homes farther from the epicenter of the dump site showed telltale signs of toxic contamination. Leaching and runoff had polluted far more than the

A security guard reads a book inside a gate that was constructed around an abandoned section of the Love Canal neighborhood.

immediate vicinity. Hooker Chemical was not the only entity that dumped waste into the old canal; reports of military jeeps carrying canisters to be buried led to further inquiries. The situation was worsened by the discovery of large quantities of the chemicals that made up the defoliant Agent Orange, which was used indiscriminately during the Vietnam War to clear the jungle so that it could not be used to shelter Viet Cong and North Vietnamese soldiers who might ambush an American advance. In 1980 chromosome damage was confirmed in eleven out of thirty-six residents of Love Canal who were tested for the genetic implications of their exposure to toxic chemicals. Love Canal appeared to be a nightmare with no end for its former residents, for the state health department, for the companies involved, and for the public at large.

THE RESPONSE TO HAZARDOUS WASTE

Love Canal unleashed the fears that Americans had repressed about the hidden costs of industrial development, but Love Canal was only the best-known of a number of sites where the toxicity of industrial by-products, particularly of the chemical industry, proved a threat to health and safety. Other sites were part of a pattern that shocked and frightened the public: sites such as the James River in Virginia, where a dangerous chemical called ketone was found in very high proportions; the "Valley of the Drums" in Kentucky, a poorly maintained landfill that housed more than seventeen thousand corroding drums of hazardous waste that contaminated drinking water for populated areas; Times Beach, Missouri; and another Hooker Chemical Company site in Michigan. Another outcry ensued. Individuals such as Lois Gibbs, who organized the Love Canal Homeowners Association to protest the predicament and to defend the rights of the people of Love Canal, typified the resistance to business as usual. A range of similar grass-roots activists challenged corporations and government. Investigative journalists eagerly covered the ensuing confrontations. Congressional committees held hearings. The toxic environment and the responsibility of corporations became an important topic of discussion at a time when faith in the American system was at an all-time low.

Love Canal and other waste sites pitted American prosperity against the very kinds of industrial processes that created it. The people who lived in Love Canal were beneficiaries of the activities of Hooker Chemical and similar companies in the Niagara Falls area. They bought their homes with the wages they earned in the production of the same kinds of chemicals that created the toxic waste buried in their backyards. It was a classic postmodern American tautology: each part of the circle of contamination could be implicated in the process of creating the contamination, all people were tragically, although not equally, culpable, and all could easily claim to be victims in one way or another. From a moral and ethical standpoint, Love Canal was a quagmire. From a legal and public policy standpoint, it was only marginally less convoluted. What soon became evident was that the American people demanded guarantees that such toxic events would be avoided whenever possible and swiftly and equitably dealt with when they could not be avoided. Governments hurried to catch up with the public; the Environmental Protection Agency was in the forefront at the federal level.

EPA AND POLITICS

At its inception, the EPA had assumed responsibility for hazardous waste cleanup, but throughout the 1970s it had moved slowly in response to mounting hazardous waste problems. The agency was very new, and the procedures for action were not yet in place. When the Love Canal story became known in 1978, the agency had not yet developed the regulations for managing such situations, first required by law in 1976. Love Canal generated a quick response from EPA. In 1979 the Hazardous Waste Enforcement Task Force (HWETF) was created with the goal of filing fifty "imminent hazard" cases—places where the mode of waste storage posed an active and imminent threat to nearby residents—in its first year. With the help of the U.S. Justice Department, which set up a small unit called the Hazardous Waste Section in the fall of 1979, the goal was achieved, showing the public, industry, and government that the task force was prepared to battle this problem. Public and congressional scrutiny continued to be great, the pressure on EPA even greater. After the election of 1980, when Ronald Reagan, widely presumed to be antiregulation and probusiness, was elected president, the pressure even initially intensified. Using an inventory of inactive waste sites derived from congressional survey data, HWETF organized an initial list of ninety-six hundred potentially toxic sites.

The crowning legal victory in the battle to assure cleanup of toxic sites occurred during the lame-duck period after Carter's defeat. The passage of the Comprehensive Environmental Response, Compensation, and Liability Act (CERCLA), more commonly known as the Superfund Act, offered the first comprehensive legal statute designed to assure the cleanup of the vast quantities of hazardous materials that had accumulated across the nation. The legislation created a $1.6 billion fund for remediation and cleanup of toxic waste sites and oil spills, financed by taxes on petroleum and other chemicals as well as by federal appropriations. The Superfund was a typically American solution: mitigation through technology, paid for by assessments on the makers of potential causes of toxicity. After a century of living with the pollution of industrialization, America had a law that offered a specific remedy entirely in keeping with the dominant value systems of the era. Under this law, polluters theoretically would be forced to repay the full cost of cleaning up after themselves.

This law resulted from the affluence and optimism of the 1960s and 1970s and set the scene for a vast battleground. Stripped of the raw fear of its consequences, toxic waste became just another quality of life issue. The questions raised at Love Canal and other waste sites were central to the future of the nation. These issues were urban and industrial, pervasive, and potentially threatening to the standard operating procedures of many industries, as well as to the quality of life of countless millions of Americans. The idea of comprehensive cleanups reflected the values of the era that was ending rather than the new "less government" promises of the incoming Reagan administration. The passage of the law on December 11, 1980, during the period between Carter's defeat and Reagan's inauguration, was ironic. It opened the way for a range of legal sanctions at the exact moment when the transition to the Reagan administration, which was far less likely than its predecessors to exercise such power, began in earnest.

Under Reagan, the federal government all but halted the accelerating enforcement of the mandate to clean up toxic waste hazards. The new administration had been elected with a very different vision of the problems that afflicted the nation, and enforcement of toxic waste laws was decidedly not a priority. The Reagan administration prescribed a new role for the EPA. The agency fell from the position of primacy it had enjoyed throughout the 1970s. When Carter-era EPA administrator Douglas Costle resigned before Reagan's inauguration on January 20, 1981, the appointment of a successor was expected shortly afterward. More than one year passed before Anne Gorsuch was nominated for the post on February 21, 1982.

During the first two years of the Reagan administration, a sharp decline in the initiation of new enforcement cases, a loss of credibility for the agency, and a drastic diminishment of morale among career employees were symptoms of the distaste with which the people of the agency viewed the goals of the new administration. A procession of weak and controversial leaders at the EPA throughout the mid-1980s also reflected these changes, and EPA, little more than a decade old, quickly lost the luster associated with its founding. No longer was this agency, with its comprehensive mission, one that Americans trusted. Instead, they watched it with a jaundiced eye.

In effect, the Reagan administration reversed the enforcement paradigm that had driven the EPA throughout the 1970s. One goal of the EPA's top leaders during this new era was the "strict conservation" of the $1.6 billion Superfund. This goal translated into a pattern of ineffectual negotiation with polluters, the initiation of far fewer enforcement suits, and almost no cleanup of toxic sites. Between January 20, 1981, and April 21, 1982, no new enforcement cases were filed by the EPA against hazardous waste sites; by September 29, 1982, only three new cases had been added. During this time more than eighteen thousand sites around the country were known to EPA to qualify for cleanup under the legal definition of Superfund. This abdication of responsibility was so great that it inspired a public outcry. The promise of EPA had been so tarnished that even prominent Republicans challenged the direction of the agency under the Reagan administration. Russell A. Train, a former administrator of the EPA in the 1970s, sharply criticized the direction of the agency and its leadership in a guest column in *The Washington Post.* Cartoonist Garry Trudeau took on the agency in his comic strip, *Doonesbury,* implying that agency administrators lied repeatedly to the public. The popular culture pillorying of EPA heightened the fear that the public retained of hazardous waste and reflected the increasing contempt with which the Reagan-era EPA was regarded. The agency founded to mitigate the fundamental by-products of the relationship between technological advancement and its ramifications and the quality of American life had lost every shred of its credibility.

EPA administrator Anne Gorsuch was toppled as much by her own lack of judgment as by public perceptions of her work, but like other Reagan-era administrators of federal agencies with responsibility for the environment, she nonetheless fell. Asked by Representative Elliott Levitas (D-Ga.), chairman of the Subcommittee on Investigations and Oversight of the House Committee on Public Works and Transportation, to produce the documents pertaining to the EPA's enforcement strategy at 160 abandoned hazardous waste sites, Gorsuch informed the chairman that President Reagan had instructed her to withhold these papers. Gorsuch also refused to turn over documents to another House panel, the Subcommittee on Oversight and Investigations of the House Committee on Energy and Commerce, headed by Representative John Dingell (D-Mich.). The president insisted that the documents in question were covered by executive privilege, a perspective that Gorsuch presented to the committee. The U.S. House of Representatives disagreed, voting to hold Gorsuch in contempt of Congress. This prompted a lawsuit by the Department of Justice aimed at quashing the subpoena served to Gorsuch.

The media pounced on the story, seeing in Gorsuch's reluctance to cooperate with Congress a potential cover-up that could match the Watergate scandal in importance. The executive privilege clause was the same one speciously invoked by the Nixon administration during the 1970s, and its use in this instance seemed suspicious. It was clear that the Reagan-era EPA had something to hide; otherwise, as went an argument that ironically mimicked Richard Nixon's view of the issue of privacy, administration officials had no need for executive privilege. Prominent media coverage followed, and the Gorsuch EPA developed what was later described as a "bunker mentality." The public sensed that an issue that was important to its quality of life was being lost in the fray, and the EPA lost what little credibility remained to it after two years of the Reagan administration.

Gorsuch was forced to resign as part of a compromise solution, but the problems of the EPA did not end. In effect, the Gorsuch era compromised the agency and made it suspect. At the end of the 1970s the EPA had been perceived as an agency with great integrity; when Gorsuch resigned on March 9, 1983, it was widely perceived as a sink of corruption and deceit, an agency that had abdicated its most important responsibility—to protect the public from hazardous waste. Even under the patient guidance of William D. Ruckelshaus, the highly respected first administrator of the agency who was called back for a second stint in an effort to shore up its lagging stature, and Lee Thomas, who succeeded Ruckelshaus in 1985, the agency failed to completely regain the public's confidence.

ENVIRONMENTAL RACISM OR CLASSISM?

As EPA floundered, other issues of toxic pollution continued to loom large over the lives of Americans. The decline in the number of high-paying jobs in the traditional industries that were the sources of much of this pollution led greater numbers of people to question the activities of some industries. Some workers had been long silenced by ignorance of the dangers, by loyalty, or by economic dependence, but as the ties between American workers and the companies that had been their sources of sustenance were rudely severed in a rapidly changing economic climate, across the nation a chorus claimed to expose the perfidy of government and industry. "Downwinders" and other civilian and military victims of radiation exposure began to demand that the nation take responsibility for the tragedies caused by exposure to nuclear and chemical material. One of the most poignant, Utah author Terry Tempest Williams, referred to her family as the "clan of one-breasted women" because of the prevalence of mastectomies among them. Her writing clearly intimated that the family's living in southern Utah was a contributing factor; one of her stories was based on the revelation that a great ball of fire that dominated her childhood dreams was actually an above-ground nuclear test flash that she saw as a child while riding in a car. Subsequent revelations in the early 1990s that the military engaged in plutonium experiments on mentally handicapped, terminally ill, incarcerated, and otherwise incapacitated individuals did little to assuage the fears of the public that one integral component of the American way of life was also the source of great harm.

Again, risk and the convenience at the core of American culture had been uncomfortably juxtaposed. Americans had always figuratively wanted to have their cake and eat it, too. They expected employment that paid well for anyone who finished high school, upward economic mobility in the course of a lifetime, and creature comforts and amenities galore. The price of such a way of living had become one of the consequences of industrialization—the ongoing search to find cheaper ways to accomplish all tasks in an effort to keep prices relatively low, keep wages relatively high, and satisfy the shareholders of the corporations that drove this process. From unannounced releases of gas from the Hanford Reservation to chemical spills in the nation's waterways, from Three-Mile Island to "Cancer Alley," the cost to individuals proved too great to bear. When Americans faced the consequences of their sense of entitlement and way of life, they typically searched for culprits. There were plenty to be found in industries and government.

At about the same time, the concept of "environmental justice" was pushed to center stage in the political debate. First brought to public attention in 1987 by the Reverend Benjamin Chavis, at the time the leader of the United Church of Christ and later head of the NAACP, the idea of environmental justice purported to show that minority communities in the United States were singled out for the siting of environmental hazards, both employment-offering industry and waste dumps, on the basis of the racial makeup of communities. It was an argument that challenged the existing strategies of large corporations as well as their motives and behavior. If demonstrable in any systematic fashion over a broad geographical area, the charges of advocates of environmental justice would prove almost as morally damaging as the institution of slavery had once been in the United States.

Environmental justice easily connected with a range of other oppositional voices in American society. It sought to dovetail two great modern American fears—nuclear and toxic poisoning—with the greatest of American injustices—racism—in an effort to regain a prominent position for civil rights issues. With the election of the Reagan administration, the traditional strategies that drove civil rights in the United States were effectively blunted. Reagan's White House was unsympathetic at best and often actively opposed the goals of the civil rights community. As the economic condition of the country worsened in the recession of 1982, whites in general became noticeably less sympathetic to the entreaties of the civil rights community. The civil rights movement needed a new strategy, and some of its leaders recognized in the idea of environmental justice an argument so compelling that it might allow civil rights to recapture the moral high ground it enjoyed during the 1960s.

The idea attracted much attention because it created a powerful moral argument in an era that devalued the arguments of moral suasion, so common in the United States since the civil rights movement, in favor of cost-benefit analysis. When leaders such as Chavis pointed to examples of the siting of toxic dumps based on racial factors, those arguments could touch any sympathies that Americans retained for the poor, the defenseless, and the wronged in U.S. society. The arguments could tap into the sentiments that the Reverend Dr. Martin Luther King Jr. so dramatically and successfully had invoked during the 1960s as he advanced civil rights as a moral issue of paramount importance in American society. Yet the environmental justice argument was more complex than King might have made. His arguments were fundamentally moral ones, aimed at the conscience of individuals and of the nation as a whole. Although Chavis utilized a moral dimension in his argument, it was woven with health and safety issues, concerns of all Americans. Unlike King, who sought equality through moral action, the environmental justice movement played to a concept of victimization. It sought sympathy and redress from this perspective, conveniently reminding other Americans that they, too, could be victimized in the same way.

The idea of environmental justice attracted much attention, but in the end it obscured the reality that the overwhelming majority of people harmed by pollution, toxic chemicals, and nuclear waste in the United States were working-class whites living near industrial plants and factories. The history of pollution had shown one irrefutable fact: people came to the "hazard," a term for the source of industrial pollution. As Love Canal showed, the genesis was often the dumping of toxic chemicals in undeveloped land that was later turned into neighborhoods. It was an equally large problem in the areas surrounding American factories. Throughout the nation, the haze of industrialization hung over the homes of European ethnic immigrants and their children in places such as the South Side of Chicago, Birmingham, Alabama, and Pittsburgh, Pennsylvania. The attorneys who specialized in siting toxic waste dumps freely admitted to a strategy, but it was not one that singled out African Americans or nonwhites in particular. Instead, they targeted populations with low levels of education, communities that were predominantly Roman Catholic, and areas where the siting of a waste facility would provide needed employment. This typically meant eastern European ethnics, Hispanics, and sometimes rural communities both white and nonwhite. From the point of view of such attorneys, African American communities were too fractious. Except in specific situations, such as those revealed by sociologist Robert Bullard in his study of Houston, it was difficult to find African Americans systematically singled out.

A kind of environmental "classism" was clearly evident. The attorneys who sited hazardous waste dumps acknowledged that some types of communities were more receptive than others. They used the often limited economic advantages of a dump to seduce such communities, admittedly seeking pliant individuals and communities to accept a greater risk than might be acceptable to the public at large. Clearly poorer communities were disproportionately affected, and some of those communities included large numbers of Hispanics and African Americans. It was equally apparent that the vast majority of people affected by toxic waste in the United States had long been and continued to be lower-middle-class whites.

NUCLEAR WASTE AND POLITICAL POWER

The process of siting the first national high-level nuclear waste dump revealed a similar set of choices on the part of the federal government. The growth in the number of active reactors led to an abundance of radioactive waste, another by-product of the concern with quality of life and the desire for cheap energy that permeated the American landscape. By the early 1980s the nation clearly needed a permanent storage facility for the growing number of spent fuel rods used in reactors across the country. This was a large and vexing problem, and the first policy reactions were directed in other areas. On December 13, 1980, the Low-Level Nuclear Radioactive Waste Policy Act was passed. It was designed to address one aspect of the waste disposal problem— the spent but still radioactive materials generated by hospitals, universities, laboratories, and similar institutions. Although policies for handling such waste were an important first step in creating a body of law that regulated radioactive waste, the law avoided the intractable problem of high-level waste, for which more stringent measures had to be provided.

The passage of the Nuclear Waste Policy Act of 1982 on December 20, 1982, was designed to remedy that problem. The law initiated a process that was designed to solve the problem of high-level nuclear material, including spent fuel rods. Under its terms, five sites across the nation were to be studied and two chosen—one in the East and the other in the West—for permanent high-level nuclear waste "repositories," as they were referred to in formal language. The basis for the choices was to be scientific; high-level nuclear waste was to be located in geological formations that could withstand any natural disaster for more than the ten thousand years required to diminish the waste material's radioactivity.

Politics quickly overwhelmed science in the decision-making process. In December 1984 the Department of Energy selected three sites to be examined for the first repository. Deaf Smith County in desolate west Texas; Yucca Mountain, about sixty-five miles northwest of Las Vegas, Nevada; and the Hanford Reservation in central Washington state were chosen. Eastern locations had completely disappeared from the initial list; they were to be considered for the second repository. Hanford and Yucca Mountain were already in use for nuclear projects. The original atomic bombs had been assembled at Hanford, and the reservation there had been a weapons-producing facility since World War II. Yucca Mountain was located adjacent to the Nevada Test Site, where above-ground nuclear tests had been conducted in the 1950s and 1960s and underground tests until the 1990s. Deaf Smith County, Texas, was remote and had few residents; the Pantex weapons plant at Amarillo, Texas, was within hours of the site by car, seemingly making area residents more amenable to the idea of a repository. All three candidates seemed to be places where opposition to a repository was likely to be minimal.

Although the Department of Energy identified twelve sites in seven states as candidates for the second repository early in 1986, the focus was already on the initial three choices. Within a few months, the DOE "indefinitely deferred" the search for the second site, leaving only the initial three sites. Protests in Texas against the choice of Deaf Smith County and the power of the Texas congressional delegation made this choice increasingly unlikely. The area around Hanford was populated, and its proximity to the Columbia River posed grave difficulties in the event of leakage in any form. That left Yucca Mountain, located in the middle of the Nevada desert and a federal weapons range in a small and politically weak state with a small population. Yucca Mountain might not have been perfect from a geological perspective, but from a political perspective it was ideal. In 1987 Senator Bennett Johnston (D-La.) and Senator James McClure (R-Idaho) introduced legislation to review Yucca Mountain among the three sites, effectively terminating the search for a location anywhere but in Nevada. Although the legislation suggested that if Yucca

Mountain was found unsuitable the other two sites would again be considered, it was clear that the process was unlikely to ever proceed that far. The combination of the record of the DOE and the vast sum of money necessary to assess the site for repository purposes, estimated at more than $1 billion in 1988, all but guaranteed that Yucca Mountain would be selected. When the legislation passed, attached to the Budget Reconciliation Act of 1987, the scientific process described in the 1982 act had become an expedient political process.

This typical exercise in power revealed much about the relationship between risk and culture in American society. Everyone was willing to enjoy the benefits of technological innovations, but when the benefits had consequences, no one stepped forward to shoulder a share of the responsibility. Whether in the case of toxic or radioactive waste, political power often determined the official response as well as the remediation strategies that were undertaken. When there was enough of a public outcry, as at Love Canal, there would be at least some effort made to protect those in the path of harm; in situations where the public was quiescent, as in the case of above-ground testing, or uninformed, as when waste leaked from industrial plants or when unauthorized radioactive emissions escaped places such as Hanford, business would continue as usual. The use of naked political power when science offered a better guide or when scientific research had not yet been conducted—Senator Johnston's Yucca Mountain legislation became known as the "Screw Nevada" bill—continued to mar the landscape. Risk seemed to count only when large numbers of people, vocal opposition, and powerful constituencies were affected. In this respect, the environmental justice movement correctly identified a phenomenon in American society; its proponents simply did not define the condition in a sufficiently broad manner.

A simple reality remained: Americans were addicted to a throwaway ethic in a consumption-oriented lifestyle and were loath to forgo it for any reason. Even when faced with the results of their own actions, they sought mechanisms to alleviate negative consequences without seriously considering the ways in which they consumed resources and consumer goods, demanded amenities, and generally lived in a mode that ignored all but the immediate consequences of their actions. Yet hazardous and radioactive waste proved that abundance had real consequences that could not be deferred. Despite myriad laws and policies, many in the nation questioned whether decisions that in effect spread the risk around were reached in any equitable manner. In a democratic society, where government responds to the dictates of the electorate, this posed a fundamental problem. For many reasons, during the 1970s and 1980s Americans lost faith in their government and its ability to protect them. The pervasive sentiment of alienation was exacerbated by the problems of toxic and nuclear waste. It seemed to many that the tools and dreams of the 1960s and 1970s failed them. This resentment of the status quo found a voice in the administration of President Ronald Reagan and especially in his secretary of the interior, James Watt.

Chapter 7

ARCH VILLAIN, HERO, OR CONSENSUS-BUSTER? JAMES WATT AND THE END OF AN ERA

In some ways it was inevitable, in others, entirely mysterious, but nothing disrupted the bipartisan political consensus of the environmental movement as much as the 1981 appointment of James Watt as secretary of the interior under President Ronald Reagan. An attorney, a staunch advocate of free-market capitalism, and a veteran of more than two decades on the losing side of a significant number of environmental battles, Watt planned an all-out assault on the reigning value system that supported the reservation of federal land, limits on the use of natural resources for the purposes of development, and the values of the environmental movement as codified in legislation such as the Wilderness Act of 1964 and the Endangered Species Act of 1973. Watt sought to turn the natural resources of the country over to those he called "the people," not the elitists who, he believed, had been managing them for the previous twenty-five years.

Watt's approach was very different than had been the norm in the office of the secretary during most of the twentieth century. His initial directives included the pronouncement that he intended to open the shallows along the scenic northern and central California coasts to offshore oil drilling as well as to declare a moratorium on the acquisition of additional land for national parks. Instead of the more traditional kind of preservation to which no less than lip service had been paid by every prior

James Watt, Ronald Reagan's secretary of the interior, attempted to shatter the bipartisan consensus in Congress that had favored the environmental movement.

post-World War II secretary of the interior, Watt emphasized the development of federally owned natural resources and the physical plants in national parks, taking credit for an initiative entitled the Park Repair and Improvement Program (PRIP) that began before his arrival. "I will err on the side of public use versus preservation," he told a March 1981 conference of park concessionaires in a statement emblematic of his philosophy. "There are people who want to bring their motorcycles and snowmobiles right into the middle of Yellowstone National Park," he is purported to have told a group of Park Service employees, "and our job is to make sure they *can.*" Watt's Department of the Interior was different from any since that of Albert B. Fall, architect of the Teapot Dome scandal of the 1920s.

But at their core, much was familiar about the ideas that Watt offered. Catering to the public to increase support was a long tradition of the agencies of the department. In the constituency-building days of the early twentieth century, the National Park Service pursued an aggressive strategy of development. Only in the 1950s and 1960s did the agency become sensitive to the ideas of preservation, in many instances only after the public dragged it toward such values as it heartily resisted. The Bureau of Reclamation built alliances with large landowners throughout the West, using public funds to provide water for agriculture and eventually for local use. Despite his cynical stance and often absurd pronouncements, Watt struck a chord with a segment of the public. His ideas harkened back to an earlier era of American conservation at the expense of the values and attitudes of the post-1945 era.

THE WATT REVOLUTION

Watt typified a strain of resentment that had deep roots in the history of the American West. A native of Wyoming, the tall, energetic, bald, and bespectacled Watt had been raised with the traditional individualistic ethic of the region that advocated development, and he had made a career of the combination of alienation, disaffection, and accepting federal largesse typical of many rural westerners. In 1980, when Republicans again took control of the White House, Watt was president and chief legal officer of the Mountain States Legal Defense Fund, a probusiness conservative think tank and publicity organization that challenged the dominance of the Sierra Club and other environmental organizations in defining the agenda for natural resource use and development. Outspoken, strident, and millennialist, Watt seemed the incarnation of the devil to the environmental movement.

Beginning with the malaise of the Carter years, the environmental movement faced problems that stemmed from its success and from its movement toward the center of the American political landscape. The combination of problems of toxic and nuclear waste gave environmentalism great credence; at the same time, the sense of long-term prosperity made possible the array of legislation such as the Endangered Species Act that resulted from the optimism of the 1960s. But by the end of the 1970s there were problems with the traditional environmentalism at the core of the bipartisan consensus that had dominated environmental politics since the late 1950s. The response to hazardous and nuclear waste came from quarters other than the core of the environmental movement. It found its voice in direct action and grass-roots protest that mainstream environmentalism had grown beyond as it focused its energy on sophisticated lobbying. Instead of urban environmentalists joining the mainstream that remained concerned with wilderness issues, a bifurcation followed.

The Democratic Congress of the late 1970s reacted slowly if at all to the changing national conditions. Dominated by representatives who gained their experience during Kennedy's New Frontier and Johnson's Great Society, Congress was tuned to the optimism of the 1960s. Beginning with the Wilderness Act in 1964 and continuing through the passage of the Endangered Species Act in 1973, Congress willingly placed limits on economic use. The lands designated under such legislation were, in the parlance of opponents, "locked up" from other forms of use. Much of Congress was willing to support Jimmy Carter's efforts to curtail expensive and wasteful projects, but the public balked when it perceived the changes as an effort to save fish and mollusks instead of as an effort to halt the wild spending of tax dollars. As jobs in a range of industries became threatened, the resources in wilderness areas and places protected by the Endangered Species Act represented potential economic development and the possibility of new jobs. It was only a matter of time until a political backlash caught up with the environmental movement.

James Watt was the embodiment of that backlash. He reflected the values of the administration of Reagan, swept into office in 1980 on a tide of resentment. As governor of California, Reagan had helped stop a U.S. Army Corps of Engineers project at Dos Rios on the middle fork of the Eel River, but his overall environmental record in the Golden State was mixed. In Washington, D.C., he sought to eliminate the environmentalist perspective that both major political parties had embraced between the middle of the 1950s and the end of the 1970s. Reagan and his administration sought to demonstrate that environmentalism did not have deep roots in American society. Instead, his administration attempted to frame environmental values as the province of an elite group with wealth who sought to restrain others from reaching similar economic objectives.

Watt also reflected the shift to the political right in the Republican Party itself. The Nelson Rockefeller-style Republicans of the early 1970s were not the same people as the core supporters of Ronald Reagan. Instead of the older-style, centrist Republican Party, the new party had moved far to the right on the political spectrum. Despite efforts during the campaign to use longtime consensus environmentalist party members such as former EPA directors Russell Train and William Ruckelshaus and former Assistant Secretary of the Interior Nathaniel P. Reed to suggest that little would change in environmental policy under Reagan, the new administration fashioned a very different approach to environmental policies than had even Republican predecessors. For positions of power in his administration, the incoming president selected people from the far right of center coalition that had supported him in the Republican primaries against the then more moderate George H. W. Bush. Watt headed the list and reflected both the agenda of the new administration and the party's movement away from the center of American politics.

In many ways, this view of environmentalism reflected the values of an earlier time. Ignoring the centrist consensus of the previous two decades, the Reagan administration espoused a view of environmentalists that more accurately described their predecessors, the conservationists of mid-century. This declaration of what at its core was class warfare, ironically perpetrated by the privileged claiming to be the dispossessed against other members of their own class, had vast ramifications for the political landscape of environmentalism.

Watt typified the kind of people well positioned for this attack. His western roots and ties gave him de facto credibility in the region that was lacked by all eastern congresspeople and in fact by anyone who was not a native of the region. Comfortable in a string tie, Jim Watt was both representation and caricature of the West. He could talk to people in rural occupations such as farming and ranching, and he was savvy enough to regard natural resource-extracting industries as powerful and valuable allies and to align his strategy with theirs. Watt built up ties between traditional users of federal land and the energy companies who sought to develop its mineral and geological resources. Instead of individuals such as Train, Reed, and Ruckelshaus, all closely identified with the centrist ambitions of the Republican Party, Watt became the characterization of the environmental perspective of the GOP.

This new secretary embarked on a concerted campaign to change the way the Department of the Interior managed its lands. He sought to rewrite most of the regulations for management within the department, remarking that the changes would be permanent because no successor "would ever change them back because he won't have the determination I do." Much of his effort focused on the deregulation of natural resources; the most dramatic changes he sought were the vast expansion of coal leasing and surface mining on Department of the Interior lands. Relying on the advice of William Coldiron, the solicitor for the Department of the Interior and a former attorney for the Montana Power Company, Watt set out to make federal resources accessible to all comers, regardless of the statutory limitations on their use.

THE SAGEBRUSH REBELLION

Watt's brand of activism reflected an aggressive campaign to alter the way government managed its lands. The Sagebrush Rebellion, promulgated out of Nevada and catapulted to national importance by Watt's ascendance, was a primary manifestation. These rebels, heir to a long tradition that argued for the return of federal lands to the jurisdiction of the states in which they were located, struck a chord in the changing West. In effect advocating a form of "states' rights," the Sagebrush rebels fashioned government from the local level up rather than from the federal level down. Beginning in the early 1970s as a response to the complaints of the Nevada ranchers who felt threatened by an increase in administrative dictates from the Bureau of Land Management, the Select Committee on Public Lands of the Nevada Legislature explored the possibility of transferring federal lands to the state. As this movement gathered momentum, its leaders saw problems with a wide range of federal statutes that seemed to these conceptual rebels to be an infringement upon their rights. Much as did the states' rights advocates of the Civil War era, the Sagebrush rebels sought a fundamental restructuring of the relations between state and federal governments. In the view of leaders such as Barry Goldwater, U.S. senator from Arizona, and John L. Harmer, the lieutenant governor of California during Reagan's governorship, the states should have more control over what went on within their boundaries and the federal government should have less. The Sagebrush Rebellion formed a figurative gauntlet for the environmental movement, dependent on federal legislation and the federal bureaucracy, to run.

This local doctrine was based largely on the idea of "culture and custom," the supposition that time-honored patterns of behavior on public land conveyed de facto ownership to longtime users. As much wishful thinking as response to an economic climate changing for the worse, this idea had no roots in any statute. The claim to federal lands in states such as Nevada was fundamentally specious; Nevada gave up its public lands as a condition of statehood in 1864, and other western states had never owned the land that was the target of claims. Typically such land had been located in the public domain. It was not local land, as Sagebrush rebels liked to insist; it was merely "locally located." In most states, BLM land—the target of most of the appropriation strategy—were lands that had fallen to that agency because no one else wanted them. Yet the strident emphasis of the rebellion articulated the fears of rural westerners and exacted the sympathy of many who had embraced the romantic mythology of the American West.

By 1981, when Reagan appointed Watt, this most recent expression of a typical western perspective was in full bloom. In 1979 both houses of the Nevada Legislature passed a bill that targeted Bureau of Land Management holdings in Nevada for transfer to the state. The bill asserted state control over mineral rights and surface access, advocated a multiple-use perspective for management, and protected existing leases made by individuals with the federal government. It made provisions to sell off land to individuals and empowered the state attorney general to pursue the transfer of the lands through legal means. The actions of the Nevada Legislature were nothing less than a revolution against the prevailing current of federal management throughout the twentieth century.

Other western politicians wholeheartedly embraced the concept. With Senator Orrin Hatch of Utah, who introduced a similar bill in the U.S. Senate in the summer of 1979, as the public leader, senators such as Dennis DeConcini and Barry Goldwater of Arizona, Alan Simpson and Malcolm Wallop of Wyoming, Paul Laxalt and Howard Cannon of Nevada, and Jake Garn of Utah all embraced the concept. Archconservatives such as Senator Ted Stevens of Alaska, Senator Jesse Helms of North Carolina, and Senator Richard Jepsen of Iowa also supported the bill as a matter of principle.

This version of the Sagebrush Rebellion was similar to previous western revolts against federal dominance of public land and, in the views of its proponents, of the economy of the West. What set this newest revolt apart was the idea that federal management in perpetuity, as specified in the Federal Land Policy and Management Act of 1976 (FLPMA), was unconstitutional; from the perspective of Sagebrush rebels, that law made the treatment of western states unequal with that of the original thirteen colonies and Texas, all of which retained control of all the land within their boundaries at the time of their admission to the Union. This shift to a constitutional and legal tactic, different from the sometimes

petulant posturing of the West, was a different strategy in the battle for an extension of the doctrine of states' rights.

As a philosophy, states' rights had been consistently discredited since the end of the Civil War in 1865. The war created a
union instead of a confederation, and little in the first seventy-
five years of the twentieth century had challenged its supremacy.
The use of states' rights arguments to oppose civil rights legislation during the 1960s further discredited this philosophy. But
the emphasis on individual rights during the 1960s, the growing
distrust of government in general and the federal government in
particular, and the plethora of environmental regulations created
a distaste for what some westerners self-righteously perceived as
a powerful federal lash.

The campaign year of 1980 was decisive for the Sagebrush
Rebellion. Wyoming, Utah, and New Mexico passed legislation
based on the Nevada bill that claimed state sovereignty over BLM
lands within state boundaries; Wyoming passed a law in which
the state claimed national forest land as well as that managed by
BLM. Arizona overrode a gubernatorial veto and passed its bill in a
general referendum. Governors Jerry Brown of California and
Richard Lamm of Colorado vetoed similar bills, while one measure in Washington state passed the legislature but was voided
by a 60 percent "no" vote in a referendum. Sagebrush Rebellion
bills were defeated in Montana, Idaho, and Oregon, but the
momentum was apparent. In 1980 Frank Church, longtime U.S.
senator from Idaho and a staunch advocate of bipartisan conservation and environmentalism, lost his reelection campaign to
Steve Symms, one of the loudest voices in the revolt. The ideas of
the Sagebrush Rebellion attracted a visible and vocal segment of
the population in many far western states as well as opponents of
federal power and jurisdiction, Libertarians and other advocates
of the fictional free market, and a range of other interests that
inhabited the fringes of the political left and right.

The rebels seemed to have found a mountain of resistance
to the ethics embodied in conservation and environmentalism. In
spite of the fact that their support was overwhelmingly rural in

the most heavily urbanized part of the country, the West, they were poised to seize legislative power and implement a political and cultural agenda that more accurately reflected the territorial era of the nineteenth century—when cattle, sheep, and mining interests dominated many western states—than any part of the twentieth. Their successes masked significant problems; ranchers were disproportionately represented in a number of western state legislatures but were hardly representative of the increasingly urban and suburban demography of many western states. Western suburbanites had little in common with ranchers and other proponents of this newly conceived states' right concept. Sagebrush rebels had to rely on mythic perceptions of the West held by people who lived in its cities and even farther away if they were to succeed in any measurable fashion. Despite such structural problems, when President-elect Ronald Reagan wired his support—a telegram that read, "I renew my pledge to work toward a sagebrush solution"—to the second conference of the League for the Advancement of States' Equal Rights in November 1980, Sagebrush rebels felt themselves riding the crest of a wave.

Reagan's support translated into immediate action. Watt's ascendance to the most important job in the nation concerning the fate of public lands sparked outrage from the environmental movement and cheers from the Sagebrush Rebellion constituency. Environmental groups long had easy access to the corridors of power; since the 1950s and 1960s representatives and senators such as Wayne Aspinall of Colorado, Alan Bible of Nevada, Clinton P. Anderson of New Mexico, Phillip Burton of California, Winfield S. Denton of Indiana, and John Sieberling of Ohio made the conservation agenda prominent. They supported the development of water resources and recreational amenities, and some could be found supporting parks and preservation as well. But the largesse they dispensed depended on a growing economy and the support of the broad coalition of social activists, government leaders, and professionals who could create solid and workable rationales for environmental objectives. Their success rested on a view of the federal government as an active and dominant force shared

by Republicans and Democrats alike, a perception that had begun
to crumble by the middle of the 1970s.

That coalition had begun with the Echo Park Dam controversy in the 1950s and the Mission 66 program of the National
Park Service, and it continued throughout the 1960s and 1970s.
Since the 1950s the bipartisan consensus had caused a revolution
in the distribution of power, wresting control of federal lands
from the commercial-use constituencies that had so dominated
the first sixty years of the twentieth century. Liberal Republicans
such as Nelson Rockefeller, whose family had been very active in
conservation since the 1920s, were essential in retaining bipartisan support for such goals, and the environmentalism of the
1960s and 1970s seemed to securely possess the center in American politics and society.

The Reagan administration's emphasis on replacing federal
services with those supplied by state and local government made
the new administration a hostile place for the bipartisan consensus on environmental issues. Watt became the agent for the
demise of the existing style. He served as the point man for a
return to an earlier form of policy-making that emphasized the
importance of local concurrence with national policy. Concerned
more with the development of federal resources by business
interests and the comfort of visitors to national park areas, Watt
turned old allies against each other and fragmented the political
structure of the environmental movement.

The business community embraced Watt's policies as a result
of fundamental changes in the American economy. The end of
the Vietnam War and the OPEC oil embargo in 1974 precipitated
a dramatic change in the American economy. The great economic
aberration—the period between 1945 and 1973, when more
Americans did economically better than ever before—neither
reflected the norm for American society nor became it. An inexorable decline in the value of real wages began along with the
oil embargo, and the age and decrepit nature of the nation's physical plant and the stagnation of American management began to
be exposed. Within five years, the decades-long upward trend in

prosperity disappeared. Industries such as automobile manufacturing, steel, and consumer electronics began to fade in response to foreign competition, interest rates rose precipitously, and the trade deficit began to grow. Natural resource industry managers who sought federal largesse in the early 1980s did so out of a sense of necessity that reflected ongoing expectations and the changing world economy.

Americans were slow to respond to the changing economy, which initially did not affect every segment of U.S. society. During the recession of 1982, when manufacturing jobs disappeared by the thousands only to be replaced with lower-paying service industry jobs that typically lacked retirement and health benefits, the widespread sense remained that this was a temporary situation rather than a structural change. The vast majority of Americans still believed that the nation would continue to increase its prosperity. They also perceived the actions of Watt's Department of the Interior as a threat to their interests.

ENVIRONMENTALISTS REGROUP

This perception spurred another response to Watt's activities: an incredible growth in membership in the mainstream organizations of the environmental movement. As a result of Watt's policies, almost every environmental group found itself with burgeoning membership lists and an expanding budget. The Sierra Club, whose membership list reached 113,000 in 1970, had grown from 178,000 to 181,000 members between 1977 and 1980. Its total for 1983 topped 346,000. The Wilderness Society membership of 48,000 in 1979 reached 100,000 in 1983 and increased to 333,000 by 1989 and almost 600,000 in 1995. The 300,000 members of the Audubon Society in 1979 became 498,000 in 1983. The broad allegiance to mainstream environmental groups reflected cultural changes in the nation, the increased importance of the many questions about the environment, and the policies of the Reagan administration.

The public responded to Watt and the policies of the Reagan administration with more vigor than leaders of environmental organizations could have possibly expected. The across-the-board growth in membership and support, the dramatic increase in donations, and the willingness to sign petitions to send to Congress created a political force that could not be ignored by most legislators. In response to the Reagan revolution, the environmental movement reached a paradoxical maturity; honed by distinct and threatening adversaries, it fashioned a sharper yet more studied approach than ever before even as its leaders were less confident of succeeding at crafting the kinds of compromises that had characterized the 1970s.

That maturity was reflected in both the increase in the number of environmental groups and the broadening range of their specific concerns. Since the Sierra Club became political in the late 1940s, it had been the overarching focus of public attention. By the 1980s there were more than one hundred major conservation groups with a range of specialized interests. Some of these, such as the Natural Resources Defense Council, experienced spectacular growth during the 1980s precisely because it saw the lawsuit and the courtroom as the best way to halt attacks on the principles of conservation and environmentalism. Founded in 1970, it had six thousand members in 1972; they became forty-five thousand by 1983. Between 1983 and 1989, in direct response to Reagan-era programs, membership grew to 105,000. The council's appeal was its willingness to litigate against seemingly unreasonable opponents within the administration. Other groups, such as the National Wildlife Federation, lost membership between 1979 and 1983, presumably to more-activist organizations.

EARTH FIRST! AND THE FRAGMENTING OF ENVIRONMENTALISM

With a newly energized but hardly manageable constituency that had grown precisely because of Watt's policies, the environmental movement broke into pieces. The result was an entire spectrum of environmental groups ranging from mainstream organizations such as the Sierra Club to fringe groups such as Earth First!, which was the first truly ecologically radical environmental group. This sometimes puzzling array of perspectives made environmental groups less cohesive as their potential power grew. By the middle of the 1980s there was a clear spectrum in the environmental movement. It began with centrist organizations such as the Sierra Club, the Audubon Society, and the National Parks and Conservation Association and extended to a very extreme periphery that encompassed groups such as Greenpeace, with its tactics of direct action, and Earth First!, which sometimes advocated "ecotage"—the destruction of property such as bulldozers that made possible environmental degradation.

With its slogan of "no compromise in defense of Mother Earth," Earth First! represented a new approach to environmentalism. Borrowing tactics from the civil rights movement and the student unrest of the 1960s, the organization encouraged a radical approach to wilderness preservation similar to that advocated by noted environmental author and iconoclast Edward Abbey in his 1975 book *The Monkey Wrench Gang*. Chaining themselves to trees, blocking bulldozers, and on occasion engaging in more-threatening tactics such as the spiking of trees with long nails that could turn into missiles if the trees were cut, Earth First! formulated aggressive action directed at its favorite targets—the federal agencies that administered land and the companies that took advantage of the favorable terms that the Reagan administration offered. "Monkey wrenching," as the more aggressive of these tactics were labeled, made confrontation in the woods as much of a psychological factor in the battle for the environment as the courtroom had become.

Earth First! was a genuine grass-roots movement, built by enthusiastic young people who scoured the nation for support. Its geographic roots were in the West, and its founders somewhat romantically saw themselves as modern-day cowboys, fighting for individuals against powerful and venal institutions. These "buckaroos," as they called themselves, were willing to go to great lengths to make their point. Earth First!'s initial appearance on the national scene occurred on March 31, 1981, when members unfurled a three hundred-foot ersatz crack painted on a black plastic tarpaulin on the face of the Glen Canyon Dam, ever a symbol to environmentalists. "Earth First!" shouted Abbey, who attended the event. "Free the Colorado [River]!" Guerrilla theater combined with an aggressive posture and the willingness to do almost anything to protect wild land characterized the organization.

Earth First! cofounder Dave Foreman, a former employee of the Wilderness Society, became the leading proponent of this philosophy. Foreman joined the Wilderness Society in the early 1970s and, in his own expression, "discovered that compromise seemed to work best." Embracing the distrust of authority that became typical during the 1960s, he affiliated with mainstream environmental organizations as a way to work for change, and after the election of Jimmy Carter to the presidency, he believed that the suit-and-tie strategy had paid off. Carter was the first avowed conservationist to live at 1600 Pennsylvania Avenue since Theodore Roosevelt. But as Foreman described in *Confessions of an EcoWarrior,* his semiautobiographical tract, "when the chips were down, conservation still lost out to industry."

Earth First! had its beginnings in the disaffection that Foreman felt at the end of the RARE II process, in which the Forest Service disappointed the environmental constituency with its recommendation that only fifteen million acres of the thirty-six million recommended in the draft of the RARE II be proclaimed as wilderness. There were eighty million roadless acres among the 190 million acres of national forest land, and wilderness advocates consented to split the category roughly down the middle. When less than one-quarter of the roadless acres made it through the process, Foreman left his position in Washington, D.C., as issues coordinator for the Wilderness Society and returned to the grassroots organizing from which he started. He began to feel that the environmental movement as a whole had moved away from its roots and his values, had replaced "Bud[weiser] and beans" with "Perrier and Brie," and had become an industry like any other instead of being an alternative approach to life on the planet. For Foreman, the replacement of Celia Hunter—an Alaskan conservationist, feminist, and World War II veteran—as the executive director of the Wilderness Society by William Turnage—who made his mark in conservation by marketing the work of Ansel Adams—was the last straw. What Turnage saw as professionalization Foreman saw as selling out.

This was the first step in a transformation that drove Foreman to a self-proclaimed extreme perspective. The moderate tone of 1970s activism seemed too subdued to accomplish much in the face of the "howling, impassioned, extreme stand set forth by off-road zealots, many ranchers, loggers, and miners. They looked like fools," Foreman remembered in the aftermath of RARE II. "We looked like statesmen. They won." Earth First!—founded by activists such as Foreman; Howie Wolke, former Wyoming representative for Friends of the Earth; Susan Morgan, former educational director for the Wilderness Society; Bart Koehler, who was the Wyoming representative for the Wilderness Society; Mike Roselle, perhaps the most political of the group; and others disgruntled with the mainstream—resulted from the sentiments Foreman expressed.

When the Forest Service's RARE II decision was made in January 1979, the bipartisan proenvironment consensus in Congress still held a dominant position. Seasoned lobbyists such as Doug Scott of the Sierra Club, an almost antithetical figure to Foreman who prided himself on working within the system, felt that environmentalism could succeed by the traditional strategy of compromise and achieve greater success than was possible from the outside. This insider tradition dated back to the Progressive era, to the very roots of conservation in the United States, and had been responsible for the overwhelming majority of conservation and environmental victories. It was a well-established strategy that promised continuous but limited success.

For the people who founded Earth First!, this was not a sufficiently satisfying goal. Earth First! began as a fringe group with the implicit ethos of countering the opposite extreme. It was a specialty taste; guerrilla theater and direct action tactics were not for everyone, but this loose organization grew in large part as a result of the ingenuity and perseverance of its dedicated core. The Sagebrush Rebellion heightened the sense that Americans needed environmental organizations on the fringe as well as in the center.

Watt's ascension gave new meaning to the idea of an organization that uses direct action as a means to its ends, and the tactics of Earth First! grew more appealing to a widening swath of the American public, in particular during the Watt years. Disillusioned by the practices of their government, a growing number of people interested in environmental issues appreciated the willingness of Earth First! to fight battles that they were willing to support but in which they were not always willing to participate.

The broadening spectrum of groups had certain advantages for the movement as a whole. As John Muir had done for Gifford Pinchot a century before, Earth First! and other direct action groups made the mainstream groups such as the Sierra Club far more palatable to industry and local bureaucrats as well as to the Reagan administration. Rather than negotiate with people such as Foreman of Earth First! or even Abbey, politicians, agency officials, and resource users could sit down with the better-dressed crowd from the Sierra Club or the Wilderness Society. This created the illusion of commonality with some environmentalists, at least when compared with the often long-haired, bearded, and extreme-sounding rhetoricians of the fringes of environmentalism. Although the mainstream environmental movement sometimes saw its extremists as an embarrassment, and although the fringe used the mainstream as a foil, the combination provided better results than either group could have achieved without the other.

During this time the environmental movement received more public attention than it had at any time in its history. Coal-leasing and timber-cutting on public lands received coverage in *The New York Times,* elevating the importance of these issues to the national news. Some environmentalists began to see their actions as akin to those of civil rights workers during the 1950s and 1960s, although such a self-serving perspective would hardly stand up to close scrutiny. Yet during the 1980s environmentalists felt themselves on the outside of political power for the first time since before the Echo Park controversy in the 1950s, and as did any other group that had experienced close ties to power for an extended period, its members had to learn new strategies to achieve their goals. Although some environmentalist insiders resented the appearance and the tactics of organizations such as Earth First!, the emergence of the fringe became a very valuable addition to what was previously a limited repertoire of tactics and approaches.

THE RESULTS OF REAGAN ADMINISTRATION POLICY

Environmentalism also benefitted from the actions of the Reagan administration. The president's appointees reflected his debt to the right wing of the Republican Party. The chemical industry provided most of the leadership of EPA, while power companies and the natural resource-extractive industries provided a significant number of high officials in the Department of the Interior. These people represented only a narrow range of the people interested in the fate of public lands, and their narrow base was reflected in the way they addressed issues. The sometimes foolish-sounding examples used by officials to support actions that looked bad to the media and the public represented one of the few times that the Reagan administration failed to clearly and persuasively communicate its positions. Watt became notorious for his loquacious public statements, but so did a range of other Reagan administration officials, in particular EPA chief Anne Gorsuch Burford and her husband, Robert Burford, head of the BLM. Although Reagan had enormous charisma and could sway the public, his department heads and agency leaders and representatives were often more abrasive.

Watt in particular became his own worst enemy. Caricatured in the media for his gleaming pate and large, round glasses, he articulated a rough-and-ready approach. In his confirmation hearings, he startled the Senate by leaving the impression that long-term planning for public lands management was futile because he expected the imminent arrival of the Messiah. To the public and the media, neither of which exhibited millennial leanings in the early 1980s, this was evidence of a clear lack of balanced judgment on Watt's part. His shaky public image worsened as he began an assault on the Department of the Interior's policies. Environmentalists challenged him in court and frequently won as the courts ruled that Watt exceeded his authority as secretary. "I Know Watt's Wrong" became a common bumper sticker slogan, and the full coffers and energized membership of environmental organizations offered clear testimony to the secretary's unpopularity.

Watt's policies drew even more ire. His efforts to organize opponents of national park policy—inholders who owned land within national park boundaries, off-road vehicle organizations, hunting and fishing groups, and others—failed as the new coalitions could muster neither the numbers nor the influence of the mainstream environmental groups. Watt proposed privatization of interpretation—the process of explaining the meaning of individual park areas to the public, within the park system, challenging both deeply held Park Service objectives and the sacerdotal and heritage function of the agency on which it based its constituency and often its importance. This, too, failed. Watt also attempted to increase timber harvests from Department of the Interior land, but he again ran afoul of the environmentally minded public. By 1983, his energy spent and his policies aground, Watt had become an immense negative for the Reagan administration.

Watt himself provided the lever that pried him from office. In the spring of 1983 he committed a final public gaffe when he announced that the membership of a Department of the Interior advisory board consisted of "a black . . . a woman, two Jews, and a cripple. And we have talent." He left office under a cloud soon after, having achieved little more than stirring up his opponents. Watt had offered a genuine and potentially damaging alternative to the bipartisan consensus responsible for so much of the environmental movement, but he lacked the diplomacy and administrative skill to permanently fracture the alliances of his opponents. Instead, he merely energized the environmental movement against him, giving it a taste of real power from the outside. Watt had raised the stakes in the environmental game, but he lacked the power to hold his hand. The results hamstrung his successors.

The first, William Clark, Reagan's chief of staff during his governorship of California who later had been appointed a California judge, was selected because of his experience and his ability to keep out of the limelight. Low key in personality and low profile in approach, Clark sought to change the image of the Reagan Interior Department left behind by Watt. He settled lawsuits out of court, made few public commitments, and generally sought to keep his department out of the headlines. Some conservationists found him friendly to their goals; Michael Frome, a longtime supporter of the national park system, determined that Clark "opened the door to conservationists that Watt had closed." Others saw him as dangerous, another Watt cloaked in a more genial, less demonstrative manner. Clark remained in office a short time, keeping the department off the front pages until after the 1984 elections and then retiring to his California ranch.

Donald Hodel became Secretary of the Interior following Clark. Hodel had been the administrator of the Bonneville Power Association from 1972 to 1978, then did a stint as Watt's number two in Interior. He rose from there to the far more prestigious and powerful position of secretary of energy. Despite his responsibility for the disastrous nuclear power program of the Washington Public Power Supply System (WPPSS), which ended in bankruptcy, he argued for "balance" in the administration of Department of the Interior resources—code words for more of Watt's prodevelopment approach now cloaked in an agreeable exterior. According to one story that circulated, Hodel met with environmentalists and drew a line down the middle of a piece of paper. The resulting columns represented places that should not be developed and those that should, Hodel told his audience. He wanted to talk about the gray areas, the places in between. To some environmentalists, this was a threatening strategy because it made Hodel's department look more reasonable than it had under Watt and because it had the potential to shatter the alliances that had grown up to fight the deposed Watt.

Hodel demonstrated this new perspective in strange ways. After a trip to Yosemite National Park in 1989, Hodel advocated dismantling the O'Shaughnessy Dam in the Hetch-Hetchy Valley

and restoring the valley to its pre-1913 condition. This gesture
would have made John Muir proud, but it seemed so eccentric in
the late 1980s that no one took Hodel seriously. Coupled with
other Hodel programs, such as his "Rayban Plan" of 1987—when
he proposed "personal protection systems" such as sunglasses,
hats, and sunscreen as an alternative to international regulations
on the emission of cancer-causing and ozone-depleting fluoro-
carbons—his remedies seemed designed to confound supporters and opponents alike.

In the end, Hodel emerged as part and parcel of the tradition
of secretaries of the interior of the Reagan-Bush era. During
Hodel's administration, Assistant Secretary for National Parks
William Horn, another Watt-era holdover, began his push to open
the Alaska National Wildlife Refuge to oil drilling. Manipulating
Native American corporations set up as part of the Alaska Native
Claims Settlement Act of 1971 and the Alaskan National Interest
Lands Conservation Act (ANILCA), signed into law by Carter after
his defeat by Reagan in the 1980 election, Hodel sought development of resources on previously secure lands dedicated by statute
to other purposes. In this, he showed the perspective of Watt with
slightly more skill at selling his message. Environmentalists
reacted with ire.

NEW REALITIES

The secretaries of the interior during the 1980s were the most visible manifestations of the change in the politics of environmentalism, but they were by no means the only such manifestations. In
other parts of the federal system, such as the Department of Agriculture, the same commodity-oriented scenarios fractured the
existing consensus. The Forest Service spent much of the decade
selling timber for one dime for each dollar's worth of cost; this
subsidy helped sustain the timber industry through difficult times,
but offered long-term stability neither to company owners nor
wage workers. It also cost the taxpayers a significant sum in an era
when many more important social and economic programs had to
beg for funds. The increased cutting on national forest lands lulled

some parts of the industry into complacency and created expectations that the Forest Service could not long fulfill. Loggers and timber industry workers believed that their jobs were secure, not understanding that they were subsidized in a way that could not be sustained. In effect, the strategy raised expectations that ran aground on issues such as the old-growth forest-spotted owl habitat controversy of the late 1980s and early 1990s.

The energized public soon entered the fray over forest use. Since the passage of the National Forest Management Act in 1976, which had come about as a result of public pressure over the change from selective cutting to clear-cutting and which had helped redefine management objectives for the agency, the Forest Service had been obligated to consider a wider range of concerns in a different manner than it had in the past. Critics continued to charge that the Forest Service placed timber above all other uses, that in essence the doctrine of multiple use, regarded by agency opponents as a justification for more timber-cutting and minimal attention to other uses, continued to hold sway. To an agency that, in the words of one of its clearest critical voices, former USFS historian David Clary, "had never abandoned the old-time religion of more-wood-for-the-nation that had blessed its birth," the National Forest Management Act offered one more way to justify its historical practices.

But the public refused to accept the way the agency made decisions. The enactment of almost every national forest plan with its myriad alternatives led to harsh criticism from a cross section of the public. At public hearings, Forest Service officials were castigated; within the agency, a group entitled "Deep Root" leaked damaging information to news media. Randal O'Toole, an economist, dissected national forest plans and showed the inadequacy of the research that supported faulty premises and conclusions. Along with other federal land management agencies, the Forest Service faced an irate public.

Earth First! honed its techniques in battles against the Forest Service. Much of its *ecotage*—an amalgam of the words *ecological* and *sabotage*—had been directed against Forest Service programs on roadless lands. That federal agency had begun what environmentalists believed was a concerted campaign to destroy the wilderness qualities of much national forest land. Roads through the center of roadless areas; timber sales at great loss to the agency, which was fortunate if it recouped one dollar in timber sales for each six spent on road-building alone; and other similar techniques convinced agency opponents that the Forest Service had declared war on wild land. Loud protests, ecotage, and other forms of resistance became common across the West throughout the late 1980s.

The conflict highlighted a war between cultures—that of the professional management agencies such as the Forest Service and that of the biocentric side of the environmental movement. In part, Watt's ascendance had called the question of the differences between the two cultures. The conflict represented the grassroots dimension of the collapse of the bipartisan consensus. As had conservationists, federal land managers believed in the ideal of progress, which in their view was tied to the concept of rational management. The environmentalists—antiscience but using scientific rationales such as biocentrism and bioregionalism as justification for their views and believing in the sanctity of untrammeled nature in a manner worthy of Muir—rejected such a utilitarian perspective. As had the Hetch-Hetchy controversy of the early twentieth century, the rise of Reagan-era philosophies highlighted differences that had been papered over in a climate of cooperation. In the more-polarized setting of the 1980s, it became easy to cling to extreme positions.

This growing partisanship reflected the growth of the environmental movement and its transformation from a relatively narrow base into the broad mainstream of American society. The environmental organizations that mobilized to stop Watt and his successors spent as much time fighting among themselves as in fighting their adversaries. They represented a wide range of interests, were specialized among themselves, and took differing viewpoints on a number of issues. Despite the differing viewpoints, these organizations exchanged mailing lists and solicited donations from each other's members.   Some environmentalists reported being contacted for membership by as many as sixty organizations in a twelve-month period. To the public, these organizations all served the same purpose, and making membership donations came to be seen as almost arbitrary. To continue to grow, many organizations had to embrace a broader array of causes, usually crossing into territory inhabited by one of their peer organizations. The environmental organizations had become prisoners of their success.

By the end of the 1980s the environmental movement had become a force to be reckoned with in U.S. society as well as in politics. James Watt could conversely take credit for the increased stature of the movement as a whole; in a reversal of Foreman's axiomatic statement about fools and winners, Watt was perceived as a character on the fringe and the environmental movement gained stature and influence. Yet the gains altered the movement, threatened its interorganizational relationships, and forced activists to recalculate strategy. As the decade ended, environmentalism in the United States had become a mainstream concern. Almost everyone professed its tenets, but most did little more than mouth those tenets. Although the environmental movement had prevented much destruction of the physical world through its various strategies, it had not developed a holistic perspective that addressed worldwide issues such as population growth and sustainability. Its maturity had been goal-directed and resulted from the circumstances of the 1980s. As issues such as increasing gaps in the ozone layer and the potential of global warming attracted the attention of the American public, leaders of environmental organizations recognized that they had to broaden their agenda to maintain the interest and support of the public and the successes of the immediate past as well as to improve the condition of the environment in the United States. Environmentalism needed to add global dimensions.

Chapter 8

EARTH DAY REVISITED:
A GLOBAL ETHOS OR A
POLITICAL PROBLEM?

At the beginning of the 1990s environmental activists had many reasons to expect a positive future. The process of containing hazardous and nuclear waste seemed to be moving toward a tenable situation; rules and regulations had been established and, despite fits and starts, had begun to be implemented. The struggles against the Reagan administration and the Sagebrush Rebellion that dominated the 1980s appeared to have been won, the Environmental Protection Agency was revitalized, and the "environment" was again a subject of widespread American and international concern. Environmentalism had become part of the belief system of a broad cross section of the American public, a concept that people widely perceived as good and for which they felt genuine respect. The 1980s had been a complicated decade for environmentalists, but one that seemed to show the way toward a broadening of environmental protection, both in the United States and abroad.

A GLOBAL ETHOS?

In the aftermath of the first Earth Day's twentieth anniversary in 1990—an international event in which people in 140 countries participated—a movement for a new global environmental ethic took shape. Spurred in part by such disasters as the

Chernobyl nuclear accident in 1986 and the erosion of the ozone layer over the South Pole and aided immeasurably by the revelations of environmental destruction following the demise of the Soviet Union late in the 1980s, this new movement was based on what its leaders considered an environmentally responsible future. Some nations, most prominently the United States, declined to participate officially in events such as the much trumpeted but largely symbolic Rio de Janeiro Summit of 1991, slowing progress and leading to a fractured dialog about the meaning of environmentalism in an international political context. But clearly a global grass-roots movement was afoot, a potential challenge to existing forms of economic, and in some cases political and national, behavior was extant. According to the most optimistic of this newest breed of environmentalist, changes in the human condition were in the offing.

Although the idea of a global environmental ethic had great currency, it masked deep tensions between the industrialized world and what economists classified as the "developing" world. These tensions seemed increasingly to pit poor Third World nations that predominated in the Southern Hemisphere with burgeoning populations against more affluent, industrial, Northern Hemisphere nations in which native rates of population growth had shrunk. In some ways, this international environmental movement coopted much of the sloganeering of the New Left of the 1960s, seeing its message as one more way to challenge both capitalism and the impact of industrialization on the physical world. As a result, nations and corporations in a position to invest in the technologies and efforts that could begin to alleviate the crisis were less inclined to do so because the rhetoric of the movement accused them of misdeeds and challenged their basic assumptions. At the same time, many Third World nations embraced industrialism as a way to bring themselves out of poverty, subjecting them to the same destructive phenomena endemic in developed nations. Even the lessons of the Soviet bloc, whose myriad environmental problems became apparent after the

Berlin Wall crumbled, did not deter some Third World nations. The result was a perplexing world in which industrialized nations pressured developing ones not to do as they had done, while the developing nations responded that industrialized societies needed to change their ways. But at the same time, the developing nations continued to advocate similar development for themselves. This became a central paradox for the environmental movement of the early 1990s.

At the core of this contradiction was the issue of population. The phenomenal growth of world population after World War II, supported by the success of strategies such as the Green Revolution, modern medical advances, and other similar techniques for improving and prolonging life, forced difficult decisions everywhere on the planet. The incredible numbers of people on the globe strained resources, continued the long-standing pattern of expanding agriculture into increasingly marginal land, and exacerbated every environmental problem that existed prior to 1945. Yet in most places, population control was difficult to achieve. Contraception remained unfamiliar to large segments of the world, medical advances helped to diminish infant and child mortality and to extend life for the elderly, and most of the preindustrial world still regarded children as an economic asset rather than a liability for families. As populations continued to burgeon, more and more habitat and wetlands—as well as standard natural resources such as timber—were devoted to their sustenance. The result was not yet doom, but a portent of a crowded, uncomfortable future. Environmental issues had become as international as the world economy. In poorly regulated international matters, it remained possible to continue a vast array of practices that damaged the physical world. Globalization meant more responsibility for Americans as they became increasingly consumed by the demands of economic survival dictated by the worsening position of the nation in the world economy. Another kind of paradox resulted: Americans, and indeed everyone else on the planet, sought a higher standard of living and a cleaner environment. No one has yet found a way to have both.

A NEW BRAND OF ENVIRONMENTAL POLITICS

American reluctance to become more involved in the global environmental movement reflected the nation's changing political climate. In the United States, a growing backlash against the environmental policies of the 1970s, shaped by the affluence of that time, began in earnest in the 1990s. In its initial phases, this backlash against the status quo once again emanated from the West. A new generation of Sagebrush rebels again attracted attention, promoting what they called the "Wise Use Movement," which coopted the turn-of-the-century rhetoric of the initial conservation movement and the tactics of the New Left of the 1960s. These advocates of individual rights above all else—and personal property rights even above individual rights—envisioned a different America, one free from the federal regulation that had so dominated the twentieth century. In their view of autonomous local communities independent of anything more than local custom and the strictures that accompanied it, they mirrored a kind of pure, preindustrial democracy that the interdependence of the late twentieth century had long rendered anachronistic.

Although in the best of circumstances the goals of the local control movement could be achieved in the governance of a small area, a number of factors precluded larger-scale replication of such experiments. The close ties of supporters of property rights to the far right—the racist, antifederal government organizations often labeled "militias" that rose to prominence in the aftermath of the April 1995 bombing of a federal building in Oklahoma City—isolated these people on the fringes of the nation. A strong sense of national investment in local places, from national parks to Bureau of Land Management areas, also mitigated against the movement's success. Although some people might see their local lands as their own, much of the rest of the nation saw them as pieces of a national patrimony.

In many ways, the internal debate about environmental policy reflected the ongoing cultural war within the United States. On one side were advocates of a paternal state, the logical outgrowth of the unbridled capitalism of the late nineteenth century writ large over the landscape of the twentieth. The bipartisan consensus on environmental issues that dominated Congress from the mid-1950s until the ascent of Ronald Reagan in 1981 reflected this value system. Opposing that side were advocates of a near-anarchic libertarianism tied to historic ideas of states' rights and, in some instances, county rights.

Beginning early in the 1990s these people banded together across the West to try to resist the plethora of environmental regulations and other mandates from the federal government. Supported by such organizations as the Center for the Defense of Free Enterprise, headed by Wise Users Alan Gottlieb and Ron Arnold—and buoyed by the National Federal Lands Conference, an umbrella organization for the local control movement, and the companies that made up the timber and cattle industries—these transplanted urbanites sought to redefine American law to suit the taste of people who made their living chiefly off federal land. Westerners offered "culture and custom" arguments that considered public land as belonging to longtime private users in a de facto manner. The result was a complicated scenario in which communities were torn apart over resource issues.

One of the earliest battles occurred in Catron County, New Mexico, which included the Gila Wilderness Area, the oldest officially established wilderness in the nation. A local couple, Kit and Sherry Laney, had purchased a 145-acre ranch, and after spending as much as $900,000 on improvements, they received permits to graze cattle on 145,000 acres of public land. Their grazing allotment covered the Gila Wilderness Area and the nearby Aldo Leopold Wilderness Area. Under existing rules, they were allowed to do this, but many—including some of their neighbors—questioned whether they had the right to graze on one thousand times the amount of land they owned. Gila Watch, a local environmental group headed by Susan Schock, herself from a ranching family, opposed the grazing of wilderness lands. A cultural as well as an economic battle ensued, highlighting the gulf between the rural West and the national consciousness.

The tension revolved over the meaning of the Wilderness Act of 1964. In the view of the national environmental community, the sanctity of wilderness areas was codified in that law. Locals thought that their economic needs took precedence and that federal land in their area was in fact county land.The Catron County Commission passed an ordinance requiring local approval of all federal regulations that applied to the county. In short, county leaders placed their jurisdiction ahead of that of the federal government.This maneuver was nothing less than a nullification argument, reminiscent of John C. Calhoun's 1830s attempts to override federal authority in the South—an argument discredited by the Civil War and the entire chain of American law since. As during the civil rights movement, advocates of local control asserted that their way of operating—according to local standards—superseded national law. Even with the memory of anti-civil rights resistance in the 1950s and 1960s that espoused similar principles, local control advocates were not dissuaded from what was a largely discredited form of construing the meaning of American law.

In 1995 the situation in Catron County remained a standoff. The Laneys continued to graze their cattle on wilderness land, and their opponents continued to seek ways to stop them. On one side were environmentalists, both local and from outside the region; on the other side were advocates of use, also local and outsiders.The fray quickly moved into the realm of politics, where influence means more than principle or ideals. New Mexico Senator Pete Domenici took the side of ranchers such as the Laneys, and former Secretary of the Interior Stewart Udall backed the advocates of protecting the designated wilderness.A typical case of the transition in American environmental politics, Catron County has vast ramifications for the future of environmentalism in the United States.

If Catron County exemplified the legal response to federal law, however specious, Nye County, Nevada, represented the extralegal response. Nye County Commissioner Richard Carver, who on July 4, 1993, drove a bulldozer at a Forest Service ranger in an effort to open a dirt road closed by the federal government and to assert local control, typified this perspective. Carver, a rancher, believed that the federal government has no right to

Dick Carver, a member of the Wise Use Movement, is shown here armed with nothing more than the U.S. Constitution in his shirt pocket.

administer land within the state of Nevada or any other state—a belief not shared by the Nevada Legislature or governor. Carver's typical response was to cite the U.S. Constitution, a copy of which he kept in his shirt pocket at all times.

Nye County was typical of the sparsely populated rural counties that embraced the Wise Use Movement. Most of the jobs in the county resulted from the Nevada Test Site or the proposed nuclear waste dump at Yucca Mountain, financed by federal money.The county received most of its funding from federal payments associated with either federal projects or federal lands, and a small minority of ranchers wielded autocratic power within the county. Places like Nye County were fiefdoms where the ruling elite, dependent on federal dollars, made all the decisions.

Carver presented himself as a moral being oppressed by the weight of an unjust federal government, but others who embraced the rhetoric of his movement in Nevada had no compunction about the use of violence to intimidate federal employees. Early in 1995, before the Oklahoma City bombing, a pipe bomb exploded outside the Forest Service office in Nevada's capital, Carson City, about 250 miles northwest of Nye County. In August of the same year, Forest Service District Director Guy Pence's van was blown up in his driveway while his wife and daughters were in the house. Sheer luck prevented their injury and possibly their death. Despite the Nye County Commission's offer of a $100,000 reward for apprehending the bomber, there was no way to discount the impact of antigovernment rhetoric in the attack. Pence was not impressed with the county's offer; he noted that it was ironic that a county that claimed that there are no federal lands in Nevada was offering federal money to clean up its reputation. Insulted, the Nye County commissioners withdrew the reward offer. One remarked, "It's [Pence's] kind of posturing that encourages violence against federal bureaucrats."

This statement unmasked the legal duplicity that was part of the core of the philosophy of the local control movement.The copy of the Constitution in Carver's pocket was a shield against change, an effort to transform the laws of the land into the tool of people with specific kinds of privilege: proximity and historic use of lands that were part of the patrimony of the American nation. Its revolt in effect a form of seizure, the county had a vested interest in disenfranchising any level of government beyond its own.This became apparent when, over the objections

District Ranger Guy Pence looks through his office after a bomb exploded outside the window behind his desk.

of the state legislature and Nevada Governor Robert Miller, the Nye County Commission chose to welcome the siting of the high-level nuclear waste dump in the county. The commission voted to accept the dump as the state fought to resist it. Enraged, the state legislature asserted its sovereignty, threatening to isolate Nye County, but the point was made: rural counties, dependent on their urban neighbors for sustenance, wanted only money from the urban areas of the states. Rural communities had ceased to see themselves as part of the same community, subject to the same laws and strictures, and instead sought to divorce their destiny from that of others in their state. It was truly a nullification argument, one that foreshadowed the possible collapse of the majority-rule principle that has governed American democracy since the beginning of the republic.

The county movement also articulated the broader range of dissatisfaction then current in the nation. There was a strident tone to such conflicts, a frustration with the standard ways of operating that had come to characterize American life. The political gridlock in the nation's capital, the failure of either party to enact fundamental change, was the focus of much of the animosity from all levels of U.S. society. A significant percentage of Americans no longer believed in their government; the Vietnam War, Watergate, the polarization of politics, the decline of standards of living, and the widespread sense of chaos all contributed to the feeling that government could not effectively solve problems. Even more disturbing, Americans had lost faith in the consensus-based form of democracy that was rooted in the Declaration of Independence and the Constitution and that had typified the twentieth century. The return to individualism, always a mythic component in American life as a way to resolve the increasing interdependence of people around the globe, was as misguided as it was understandable. Nostalgia for a lost American way of life— when the "little guy," as the archaic phrase had it, was important— was easy to muster as the nation's economy reshaped to meet the demands of the marketplace. In this comprehensive restructuring, hundreds of thousands—from factory workers in the 1970s and 1980s to corporate managers in the 1990s—found themselves jobless and unable to find new employment at a comparable wage. Individualism made a wonderful psychic antidote to the problems of economic interdependence.

Frustration came to fruition in the 1994 off-year congressional elections, when a "throw the bums out" mentality pervaded the electorate. Incumbency became a disadvantage as a group of representatives, led by the conservative gadfly Republican Newt Gingrich of Georgia and supported by seventy-three incoming freshmen congresspeople, swept the long-standing Democratic majority from the House of Representatives. The 102nd Congress proclaimed a mandate, the creation of a new America in which property rights were to be respected and federal government would not meddle in the lives of ordinary people. These two seemingly linked ideas were far more diverse than the people who subscribed to this point of view imagined.

The populist nostalgic tone of this rhetoric was seductive. It promised a return to the old ways, when the United States dominated the world and America was the engine that drove the planet's economy. In this formulation, the only obstacles were ones unduly placed in front of the American people by malevolent forces that sought to impinge upon their individual rights. The rules constricting economic success would be stripped away, and Americans could return to the idyllic prosperity that many believed they had once enjoyed.

CHALLENGING THE REGULATORY STATE

One of the targets of this dissatisfied constituency's ire was the plethora of environmental regulations that had multiplied since the end of World War II. Antipollution legislation such as the Clean Air Acts, proclamations of new national parks and other legislation that in the parlance of opponents "locked up" valuable natural resources from development—and most of all, the Endangered Species Act—were targets of legislation that sought to dismantle protections that had become an integral part of the American political landscape.

During the first year following the seating of the 102nd Congress, nearly every federal land management agency came under attack. The National Park Service was ordered to create a list of parks that could be decommissioned; drilling for oil again threatened the Alaskan National Wildlife Reserve; instead of the typical multimillion-dollar budget that new parks receive, the California Desert National Park in the Mojave Desert was given an appropriation of one dollar for fiscal 1995–1996; and the Endangered Species Act was renewed, but only after prolonged debate and a considerable weakening of its provisions. Privatization of federal resources, from grazing land to timber, became the watchword of the day.

In a manner similar to former Secretary of the Interior James Watt's assault on bipartisan consensus a decade earlier, this new emphasis on individualism drove a wedge into the values of the environmental movement. Intrinsically tied to the idea of the federal government as arbiter of disputes and regulatory power, the environmental movement faced a major problem. Sixty years after the New Deal and nearly thirty after the Great Society, a significant percentage of Americans no longer believed that national government was the best arbiter in American society. A vocal percentage of Americans, partly romantic and partly frustrated, longed for the way they remembered life being before the national government seemed to be "on their back," as the phrase went. Rather than the protector of people, government had acquired the reputation as an oppressor.

The changing economic climate that had made life harder for the American middle class and increased government regulation seemed to be the sources of people's woes. Oregon loggers blamed the demise of the state's timber industry on the Endangered Species Act, which in part protected the habitat of the spotted owl. This land consisted of the acreage that contained the last of the state's old-growth forest. As had workers in many traditional industries, by 1975 loggers and mill workers were experiencing a level of insecurity they had not felt since before World War II. They reacted to this insecurity by blaming the spotted owl.

This reaction was predictable but fallacious. The small area of old-growth forest that was owl habitat would hardly have revived the dormant Oregon forestry industry. By the early 1990s major timber companies had shifted their main base of cutting to southeastern forests, following the cyclic pattern of timbering that drove the changed industry. No longer were these companies family- or regionally owned; the great corporate takeovers of the 1980s had made most timber companies subsidiaries of large multinational conglomerates. Many companies were also saddled with debt as a result of these takeovers, forcing them to work on a smaller percentage of profit. The result was the marginalization of portions of their workforce, which included downsizing, layoffs, and poorer-paying jobs. Inevitably, the people whose lives and livelihood were affected reacted with frustration.

By the 1990s the memory of the way life had been in the United States before the advent of environmental legislation had begun to fade. Few remembered the reasons for environmental regulation: the widespread pollution of the air, the skies, and the water that was the legacy of industrialization; the soapsuds from detergents that marred waterways; the dumping of raw sewage into lakes and rivers; and the great clouds of haze that hung over industrial communities. Even the famed 1970s song by Marvin Gaye, *Mercy, Mercy Me (The Ecology)* contained the phrases: ". . poison in the air and in the sea, fish full of mercury and radiation in the forest and in the sky, animals and birds live near by . . .," was remembered for its music and not for the message in its lyrics. Environmental regulation had been responsible for a cleaner, better environment by the 1990s. Journalists such as Gregg Easterbrook, author of *A Moment on Earth: The Coming Age of Environmental Optimism,* saw success in the results of the environmental revolution and a clear charter to a less destructive future. Americans, and indeed the world, had learned lessons, people such as Easterbrook believed, and the future would be better as a result.

This belief was both encouraging and potentially dangerous. There was no doubt that a generation of environmental regulations had made the United States cleaner and had begun the process of protecting people from hazards to their health and the world they lived in from widespread degradation.Advances in science meant more-comprehensive analysis of environmental change as well as a greater understanding of the impact of previous human activities. But success in the 1990s was not the end of the battle; the past's policies had to continue if the gains of the environmental movement were to be retained.

In this sense, Easterbrook in particular offered a threatening message. He pointed to the doomsday dimension of environmentalism as the source of one kind of problem. Environmentalists routinely implied that the immediate end of life as humans knew it would result from this or that activity. Easterbrook's message was that the success of environmentalism—from the reforestation of New England in the twentieth century to the return of a wide range of plant and animal species—closed a chapter in the history of the nation.The urgency had worn off, Easterbrook seemed to imply, and the need for immediate action had passed.

Although Easterbrook himself supported environmental protection, his message could be construed as a list of reasons for ceasing to protect the environment; his words could be read as meaning that the job was completed and that further regulation was unnecessary and undesirable.There were elements in American society to whom this interpretation was not only important, but also essential. Some people believed that the "doomsday lobby," as environmentalists were referred to by some opponents, had been wrong about everything but had succeeded in swaying an easily led public. Intentionally or otherwise, Easterbrook gave such arguments the support they needed.

More problematic was the so-called Republican Revolution, with its stated objective of decreasing the power of federal government in the lives of the American people. Even though it became obvious that "big government" in the New Deal sense was becoming anachronistic and that rules and regulations placed boundaries on nearly every aspect of American life, there was still great value in the idea of shared spaces, such as public lands, and a shared commitment to a cleaner and safer environmental future. The mechanism for accomplishing such goals had always been provided by the national government. From the point of view of the environmental movement, the mandate that Republican congressional officials claimed for themselves was a disaster.

By the end of 1995 the assault on bipartisan environmentalism had begun to waver. Despite the noisiness of a range of congresspeople—including Representative Jerry Lewis of California, who sought to restrict the funding for newly established national parks, and others such as Representative Helen Chenoweth of Idaho, who wanted to dismantle national forest protection through "logging without laws" timber legislation disguised as a salvage rider to an appropriations bill—this movement encountered the opposition of the urban public. Intellectually and emotionally, much of the American mainstream was sympathetic to the idea of local control. When the millions of urban Americans who enjoyed the outdoors discovered that their sympathy for that idea could result in the dismantling of their great outdoor playgrounds—the places they loved to hunt, fish, or just relax—a backlash against the local control movement began. With the help of celebrities such as Robert Redford, who lent his name to environmental causes, and newly revitalized environmental groups, who once again benefitted from the perception of an attack on the environment by special interests, the public began to see the local control movement for what it really was: a form of elitism that sought, in the guise of protecting private property, to lock up valuable resources from public use. In effect, the public began to recognize that the Wise Use Movement was exactly what it claimed its opponents to be: a special-interest group that sought to claim a part of the inheritance of all Americans for a very small and very vocal group.

A WORLD WITHOUT A CENTER

The sociopolitical climate in the United States during the middle of the 1990s did not lend itself to consensus-building. Instead, polarization was the watchword of the day. The middle of the political spectrum seemed to crumble against both extremes, making resolution through consensus an unlikely prospect. The polarization was especially dramatic in the battles over the environment. To partisans on both sides these were life-and-death battles in which compromise was more than impossible—it was an abdication of moral responsibility.

In this sense, environmental protection had become a litmus test, in the manner of abolitionism in the mid-nineteenth century or abortion in the 1980s and 1990s. This forced dichotomy alienated people between the extremes, and those on both sides who sought consensus for entreaties that searched for creative and balanced solutions often found their efforts rejected out of hand by both sides. This created a dilemma that seemed increasingly unresolvable.

By the time the 1996 presidential campaign began, Americans had definite sentiments about the environment. Poll after poll demonstrated that Americans cared about their surroundings and sought to protect them. Equally, many studies showed that Americans placed their economic objectives above their environmental concerns. They were prepared to support sacrifice in the name of environmentalism as long as someone else made the sacrifice. This evidence offered a typically national paradox that pitted Americans' beliefs and their sense of the world against the hard, cold realities of life in a culture that above all else valued acquisitiveness and convenience and saw conspicuous consumption as part of its birthright. This bifurcation showed the great success of the environmental movement in the post-World War II era as well as its enormous shortcomings. Environmentalists had succeeded in persuading the majority of Americans of the value of protecting the environment. They had not resolved the fundamental tension between the cultural and individual restraint that this ethic of protection requires and the acquisitiveness and individualism that has been the hallmark of the nation during most of its first two hundred years.

The circumstances of the 1990s posed a major question for the environmental movement. Although protections were in place that made the air and water cleaner and the environment less toxic than it had been twenty years before, and although as a result of a century of conservation, there were more trees in 1995 than there had been in 1895, leaders of the movement had to ask themselves if the ethic they embraced had really taken hold in American society. To be sure, environmentalism had become part of the nation's popular culture, encoded into the messages of everything from children's television programming to beer commercials, but it was a reflexive environmentalism, a popular icon regarded as a "good" that required little effort or thought. Despite the value of public opinion and knee-jerk public support, activists had to ask themselves if this popular environmentalism was really sufficient to accomplish the goal of a more sustainable environment. It was a question that few environmentalists could answer in an affirmative fashion.

This was the paradox of the rise of environmentalism in the post-World War II era. Environmentalism had emerged from the conservation movement and become a mainstream mass movement; it had achieved remarkable, if not always comprehensive, results. By the 1990s the signs of its triumph were everywhere. The American environment was cleaner than it had been before the environmental revolution. Rules and regulations protected desert tortoises in development-crazy Nevada and spotted owls in Oregon. Urban residents no longer had to endure smoke-filled skies. Leaded gasoline was almost a memory. Americans could claim significant success in the battle against the by-products of their economic prosperity.

But the greening of the nation was far from complete. The environmental movement failed in two distinct ways: it never entirely shed its privileged-class origins, and by becoming a mass movement that American popular culture embraced, it eviscerated itself. Nor were environmentalists able to connect in meaningful ways with global protection efforts. The discourse of the international movement failed to resonate with the American public. In the middle of the 1990s American environmentalism had run up against itself, a victim of its own successes. Its limitations were the function of the perspectives that most environmental leaders shared and of the class from which they emanated. Popular culture mass movements meant that people paid lip service to the concepts of environmentalism without engaging in the behaviors necessary to turn concepts into action. The greening of the United States had begun, but it was sidetracked. The groundwork for environmentalism had been done, and the legislation to support it had been in effect since mid-century, but its effect on the behavior of Americans remained minimal. Even after more than forty years of success in government actions, the United States could not refer to itself as a "green nation." The foundation had been laid, but long-term success clearly required different strategies.

In this respect, the Earth Day celebrations of the 1990s typified the nation's half-hearted environmentalism. The pageantry masked a tenuous commitment. Earth Day worked as symbol but not truly as a call to action; on the twentieth anniversary of the first Earth Day in 1990, more than two hundred thousand people showed up in New York's Central Park to celebrate their commitment to the environment. Together they created almost forty-five tons of refuse; it is entirely possible that the planet might have been better off if they had just stayed home. It was too easy for Americans to pay homage to the idea of environmentalism without implementing its principles in their lives. In an era when the concept of "rights" had entirely overwhelmed the concept of "responsibilities," the celebratory hollowness of Earth Day reflected the limits of environmentalism in the United States. On an intellectual level the "greening" of the United States had definitely begun; Americans embraced the concept wholeheartedly in their popular culture and education. In action the greening of the nation was only the beginning; people routinely professed environmentalism but equally as routinely failed to practice it.

BIBLIOGRAPHY

Abbey, Edward. *The Monkey Wrench Gang*. Rev. ed. Salt Lake City: Dream Garden Press, 1985.

Ambler, Marjane. *Breaking the Iron Bonds: Indian Control of Energy Development*. Lawrence: University Press of Kansas, 1990.

Brick, Phillip, and R. McGreggor Cawley, eds. *The Land Rights Movement and Renewing American Environmentalism*. Lanham, MD: Rowman & Littlefield, 1996.

Brown, Michael. *Laying Waste: The Poisoning of America by Toxic Chemicals*. New York: Pantheon Books, 1979.

Bullard, Robert. *Dumping in Dixie: Race, Class, and Environmental Quality*. Boulder: Westview Press, 1990.

Carson, Rachel. *Silent Spring*. New York: Fawcett Crest, 1962. Cawley, R. McGreggor. *Federal Land, Western Anger: The Sagebrush Rebellion and Environmental Politics*. Lawrence: University Press of Kansas, 1993.

Cohen, Michael P. *The History of the Sierra Club, 1892-1970*. San Francisco: Sierra Club Books, 1988.

Clary, David A. *Timber and the Forest Service*. Lawrence: University of Kansas Press, 1986.

Colten, Craig E., and Peter F. Skinner. *The Road to Love Canal: Managing Industrial Waste Before EPA*. Austin: University of Texas Press, 1996.

Culhane, Paul. *Public Lands Politics*. Baltimore: Johns Hopkins University Press, 1981.

D'Antonio, Michael. *Atomic Harvest: Hanford and the Lethal Toll of America's Nuclear Arsenal*. New York: Crown Publishers, 1993.

Dasmann, Raymond F. *The Destruction of California*. New York: Collier Books, 1965.

Dunlap, Riley, and Angela Mertig, eds. *American Environmentalism: The US Environmental Movement, 1970-1990*. New York: Taylor & Francis, 1992.

Dunlap, Thomas R. *DDT: Scientists, Citizens, and Public Policy*. New Jersey: Princeton University Press, 1981.

Foreman, Dave. *Confessions of an Eco-Warrior*. New York: Harmony Books, 1991.

Freemuth, John. *Islands Under Siege: National Parks and the Politics of External Threats*. Lawrence: University Press of Kansas, 1991.

Frome, Michael. *Regreening the National Parks*. Tucson: University of Arizona Press, 1992.

Goldsteen, Joel B. *Danger All Around: Waste Storage Crisis on the Texas and Louisiana Gulf Coast*. Austin: University of Texas Press, 1993.

Gottlieb, Robert. *Forcing the Spring: The Transformation of the American*

Environmental Movement. Washington: Island Press, 1993.

Graf, William L. *Wilderness Preservation and the Sagebrush Rebellions.* Lanham, MD: Rowman & Littlefield, 1990.

Hardin, Garrett. *Nature and Man's Fate.* New York: Holt, Rinehart and Winston, 1959.

Hardin, Garrett. *Exploring New Ethics for Survival: The Voyage of the Spaceship Beagle.* New York: Penguin, 1972.

Harvey, Mark W. T. *A Symbol of Wilderness: Echo Park and the American Conservation Movement.* Albuquerque: University of New Mexico Press, 1994.

Hays, Samuel P. *Beauty, Health, and Permanence.* New York: Cambridge University Press, 1987.

Hirt, Paul. *A Conspiracy of Optimism: Management of the National Forests Since World War II.* Lincoln: University of Nebraska Press, 1994.

Hundley, Norris, Jr. *The Great Thirst: Californians and Water, 1770s-1990s.* Berkeley: University of California Press, 1992.

Hurley, Andrew. *Environmental Inequalities: Class, Race, and Industrial Pollution in Gary, Indiana, 1945-1980.* Chapel Hill: University of North Carolina Press, 1995.

Jackson, Kenneth T. *Crabgrass Frontier: The Suburbanization of the United States.* New York: Oxford University Press, 1985.

Lewis, Martin W. *Green Delusions: An Environmentalist Critique of Radical Environmentalism.* Durham, NC: Duke University Press, 1992.

McPhee, John. *Encounters with the Archdruid.* New York: Farrar, Straus, and Giroux, 1970.

Melosi, Martin V. *Pollution and Reform in American Cities, 1870-1930.* Austin: University of Texas Press, 1980.

Mintz, Joel A. *Enforcement at EPA: High Stakes and Hard Choices.* Austin: University of Texas Press, 1995.

Nash, Roderick. *Wilderness and the American Mind,* 3rd ed. New Haven: Yale University Press, 1982.

Norton, Bryan. *Toward Unity Among Environmentalists.* New York: Oxford University Press, 1991.

Paehlke, Robert C. *Environmentalism and the Future of Progressive Politics.* New Haven: Yale University Press, 1989.

Perlin, John. *A Forest Journey: The Role of Wood in the Development of Civilization.* Cambridge: Harvard University Press, 1989.

Ponting, Clive. *A Green History of the World.* New York: Penguin, 1991.

Pulido, Laura. *Environmentalism and Economic Justice: Two Chicano Struggles in the Southwest.* Tucson: University of Arizona Press, 1996.

Pyne, Stephen J. *Fire in America.* New Jersey: Princeton University Press, 1982.

Radford, Jeff. *The Chaco Coal Scandal: The People's Victory Over James Watt.* Corrales, NM: Rhombus Publishing Company, 1986.

Reisner, Marc. *Cadillac Desert: The American West and Its Disappearing Water.* New York: Viking, 1986.

Rhodes, Richard. *The Making of the Atomic Bomb.* New York: Simon & Schuster, 1988.

Rhodes, Richard. *Dark Sun: The Making of the Hydrogen Bomb.* New York: Simon & Schuster, 1995.

Rosenbaum, Walter A. *The Politics of Environmental Concern.* Westport, CT: Praeger Publishers, 1973.

Rothman, Hal K. *On Rims and Ridges: The Los Alamos Area Since 1880.* Lincoln: University of Nebraska Press, 1992.

Sheffer, Victor B. *The Shaping of Environmentalism in America.* Seattle: University of Washington Press, 1991.

Simon, Julian L. *Population Matters: People, Resources, Environment, and Immigration.* New Brunswick, NJ: Transaction Publishers, 1990.

Simon, Julian L., and Herman Kahn, eds. *The Resourceful Earth: A Response to Global 2000.* Santa Cruz, CA: Blackwells Press, 1984.

Udall, Stewart. *The Quiet Crisis.* New York: Holt, Rinehart and Winston, 1963.

Whorton, James. *Before Silent Spring: Pesticides and Public Health in Pre-DDT America.* New Jersey: Princeton University Press, 1974.

Worster, Donald. *Rivers of Empire: Water, Aridity, and the Growth of the American West.* New York: Pantheon Books, 1985.

Yergin, Daniel. *The Prize: The Epic Quest for Oil, Money, and Power.* New York: Simon & Schuster, 1991.

Zakin, Susan. *Coyotes and Town Dogs: Earth First! and the Environmental Movement.* New York: Viking, 1993.

CREDITS

INDEX